£4 50

THE
PRICE GUIDE TO
DOLLS

Antique and Modern

Constance Eileen King

Published by

THE ANTIQUE COLLECTORS' CLUB
5 CHURCH STREET
WOODBRIDGE
SUFFOLK

Frontispiece: see page 6.

Printed in England by Baron Publishing,
Church Street, Woodbridge, Suffolk.

FOREWORD

The Antique Collectors' Club, formed in 1966, pioneered the provision of information on prices for collectors. The Club's monthly magazine *Antique Collecting* was the first to tackle the complex problems of describing to collectors the various features which can influence prices. In response to the enormous demand for this type of information the *Price Guide Series* was introduced in 1968 with **The Price Guide to Antique Furniture**, a book which broke new ground by illustrating the more common types of antique furniture, the sort that collectors could buy in shops and at auctions, rather than the rare museum pieces which had previously been used (and still to a large extent are used) to make up the limited amount of illustrations in books published by commercial publishers. Many other price guides have followed, all copiously illustrated, and greatly appreciated by collectors for the valuable information they contain, quite apart from prices.

Club membership, which is open to all collectors, costs £6.95 per annum. Members receive free of charge *Antique Collecting,* the Club's monthly magazine, which contains well-illustrated articles dealing with the practical aspects of collecting not normally dealt with by magazines. Prices, features of value, investment potential, fakes and forgeries are all given prominence in the magazine.

In addition members buy and sell among themselves; the Club charges a nominal fee for introductions but takes no commission. Since the Club started many thousands of antiques have been offered for sale privately. No other publication contains anything to match the long list of items for sale privately which appears monthly.

The presentation of useful information and the facility to buy and sell privately would alone have assured the success of the Club, but perhaps the feature most valued by members is the ability to make contact with other collectors living nearby. Not only do members learn about the other branches of collecting but they make interesting friendships. The Club organises weekend seminars and other meetings.

As its motto implies, the club is an amateur organisation designed to help collectors to get the most out of their hobby; it is informal and friendly and gives enormous enjoyment to all concerned.

For Collectors – By Collectors – About Collecting

The Antique Collectors' Club, 5 Church Street, Woodbridge, Suffolk.

ACKNOWLEDGEMENTS

I would like to acknowledge the help given in obtaining photographs from Christie's South Kensington by Susie Mayer and Lindsey Cooper. At Sotheby's, Charles Walford kindly allowed photography in the saleroom, while Richard Lane of Phillips also allowed items to be photographed during viewing. Without the willing co-operation of the staff of these salerooms, the book would not have been possible. I also thank Richard Wright and Mrs. Beatrice Wright for their help and photography and my husband, who cast an accountant's eye over my quoted prices.

C.E.K.

Frontispiece

German Bisque Headed Doll
Marked 'S&H 1248'. c.1910. Height 43cm:17in.

German dolls depend greatly on the quality of the features; in this example they are well defined, with raised shaping of the brows. The original wig is worn and the mouth is modelled in an open position and with teeth; the eyes are sleeping. The body is of the heavy quality jointed type and an attractive blue coat of soft wool decorated with silk motifs is worn with a matching bonnet and motoring veil, creating an attractive period piece. The doll wears a cream silk dress and the original underwear, and the ears are of the pierced type common to many of the better German dolls such as this Simon and Halbig.

£150

Courtesy Phillips

6

CONTENTS

PRICE REVISION LISTS

Annually in May — the first will be published in 1978

In order to keep the prices in this book fully up to date, the publishers prepare annually a Price Revision List for changes in values up to 1st May each year. This is available by the end of May and costs £1.35 by banker's order which is enclosed with this book or £1.45 cash with order form.

ANTIQUE COLLECTORS' CLUB
5 CHURCH STREET, WOODBRIDGE, SUFFOLK

INTRODUCTION

Dolls, perhaps to a greater extent than any other small collectable items, have escalated rapidly in price over the last two years and ordinary pieces that were sold for £20-£25 some three years ago now fetch £100-£130. Surprisingly, some of the early and rarer examples have risen in price only in pace with inflation, and it is mainly among the more mundane products that the huge price increases are witnessed. The weakness of the pound in 1976 meant that Continental dealers scoured Britain for dolls and prices obviously rose sharply; this mad buying period has now calmed, as the pound has regained some of its value and prices are noticeably stabilising.

This Price Guide is based on amounts paid, mainly by dealers, in the London salerooms over the past two years. Maverick prices, where two collectors or dealers vie with one another for a piece and pay a price quite out of line with the current trend, are ignored, so that the prices quoted are not necessarily those actually realised.

Fashions in collecting have had a strong influence on prices recently and some not uncommon types of doll have enjoyed sudden bursts of popularity, such as the Simon and Halbig Orientals, which peaked in price and are now on a comparative decline. At the time of writing, Kämmer and Rheinhardt jointed characters are fetching surprisingly high prices but, as more appear in the salerooms, they might also settle into a slightly lower range. Where saleroom prices are linked closely to the American values, as in Googlie-eyed dolls, it is very unlikely that prices will drop.

American dealers discriminate to a far greater extent than the British between types of dolls made by individual makers, so that the variations of price seen in the States are even more subtle. There has been a strange unawareness of quality in many of the prices fetched in London, so that a poorly tinted Jumeau, made of an indifferent and even unpleasantly textured bisque, often fetched as much as a fine example. When sold by dealers, these differences would, of course, be reflected but they are certainly not mirrored to any great extent in the salerooms, where a mere mark often sets the price within £20-£50. With the greater sanity of the strengthening pound, more discriminating prices should again result.

Damaged dolls are always difficult to evaluate but are not as comparatively worthless as, for instance, a piece of porcelain, as even if the doll's head is broken the body still has a spare part value. The prices paid for badly cracked dolls have however increased significantly recently, though they are avoided by collectors and mainly bought by the trade for restoration. There is little interest in the cheaper German dolls that are at all damaged, as these are not worth the high cost of restoration. The value of a restored head is also problematical, though I tend to value them as very little more than the original damaged doll.

Reproduction and artist-made dolls are beginning to appear now in Europe as well as the States. The bisques made in America are particularly effective, though the painting of the eyes often leaves something to be desired. In Britain there are several makers all working towards a well-produced quality figure, whether in wax or china, though it is at present impossible to assess their long term potential value. It was considered a few years ago that, as porcelain and bisque dolls became more expensive, the more impecunious collectors would turn to the early compositions, wood-flours and even plastic dolls; fortunately this has not happened in Europe and the new collectors seem content to buy fewer antique dolls rather than pieces that could have come from the toy boxes of their own childhood. In America much more recent dolls have a value and the collectors will often mix the finest and most expensive antique dolls with the plastics of the 60s. It is here that one of the main differences between the American and European approach is evidenced, the Europeans collecting 'antique dolls' and many Americans 'dolls'.

Some of the more basic dolls quoted in this salesroom-based guide can in fact be purchased for a lower price from dealers even in London itself, a situation engendered by the presence of Continental dealers. At a Sotheby's sale in the summer of 1977 for instance, Armand Marseilles, in need of rewigging and costuming, were fetching more than well restored examples in shops, a situation which is also seen in other antiques at present and which makes trading very difficult for the native dealer.

The whole state of the doll market is at present very much in flux. A lot of new dealers and collectors have appeared, feeling no doubt that they are 'on to a good thing', while other small collectors and dealers who have sold a few dolls alongside their general antiques have dropped out, feeling that the common dolls have become overvalued. The sensible collector buys what he or she likes, and avoids being too much influenced by collecting fashions, as buying a not uncommon item at its height of popularity is a sure means of making a poor long term investment.

C.E.K.

CHURCH RELATED FIGURES

Nativity scenes have been assembled in churches since the sixteenth century. At first the intention was instructive and the peasantry was shown, in tableau form, a story that it was incapable of reading. By the eighteenth century the lofty motivation of the early assemblers was largely lost, and churches, merchants and princes competed to own the largest and finest scenes. Great ladies sometimes used costly fabric, cut from dresses in their wardrobes, to dress the figures lavishly. Mary, Joseph, Jesus, the three kings and the shepherds, who had formed the original group, were added to, until shops and shopkeepers, animals, buildings, scores of angels and ladies and gentlemen of the court all combined towards an opulent effect. These figures were made in such large numbers in Italy and Germany that they come on to the market quite frequently but suffer as to the price they command, as they are not quite fine enough to be classed as works of art and sold in sales of statuary, nor are they quite in the doll collecting sphere, though it is in these sales that they usually appear.

The heads are made of terra cotta or wax and range greatly both in quality and attractiveness. Generally, one in the form of a woman with a sweet face will sell for much more than a man, whose face, with wrinkles and warts, might be modelled with more actual skill, but does not appeal to the doll collector. In relation to almost any other type of figure, they are considerably undervalued and could form a very worthwhile collecting field for the more impecunious.

Costumed statuettes, in wax, of the Infant Jesus or the Virgin Mary, were sometimes given as gifts to stand in the nursery or schoolroom. Some examples are quite horrific and were obviously meant to chasten, while others have gentle expressions and are often bought for inclusion in doll collections. The swaddling babies, that were given as gifts at a child's christening, are much more obviously playthings. These usually find eager buyers, though again quality varies greatly, from the roughly carved and crudely painted babies to others that were elaborately made in poured wax and skilfully costumed in fine fabrics. They can range in value from about £5 upwards.

Crèche figure
Unmarked. c.1700. Height: 39cm:15½in.

A lady doll from a crèche setting. The crèches were assembled in churches and sometimes in palaces to illustrate the worshippers at the birth of Christ. People from all stations in life were included, from peasants to wealthy court ladies, such as this figure seen here with her head reverently bowed. The head is made of terra cotta, realistically decorated in paint, a decoration that has often flaked away and spoiled the appearance. In this example the painting of the face is still in very acceptable condition, as is the applied wig. From the waist down, the figure is composed of a canvas-covered wire frame. The delicate terra cotta hands are in a very damaged condition, but the costume is good, especially considering that the date given above is highly conservative and that the model probably dates from the late seventeenth century. These crèche figures, though often included in doll collections, are very much on the border line between dolls and statuettes and consequently prices are very low in relation to their age and obvious artistic merit.

£40 – £50

Church related figure
Unmarked. 18th century. Height 36cm:14in.

A particularly beautiful carved and painted figure of Bavarian origin possibly intended to represent the Infant Jesus, as the fingers of the right hand, now broken away, were raised in blessing. The wool wig applied to a canvas base is typical of those used by the nuns, who often costumed these doll-like figures freshly each year. In this case the costume is roughly made and fairly recent. The carving and articulation of this figure is quite superb and the feet are robustly carved with great animation and to a standard never found on play dolls. These figures were originally very costly and dressed in the finest brocades and silks with applied semi-precious stones. Their superb craftsmanship is often hardly reflected in the price they obtain in Britain, though this example was so obviously impressive that a reasonable figure was reached.

£200

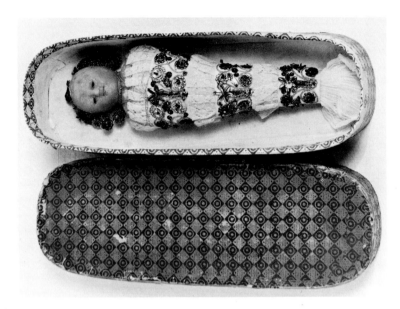

Swaddling figure
Unmarked. c.1825. Height 25cm:10in.

A particularly fine example of a poured wax swaddling figure of the Infant Jesus. The doll is in superb original condition and enclosed in a matchwood box covered with printed paper. The box carries an inscription to the effect that it was given as a gift in 1825. These figures were popular christening or birth gifts, though more popular in European countries than in England. The wax lids half cover the doll's black iris-less eyes, the mouth smiles slightly and the hair is moulded to suggest a centre parting. The body is encased in highly decorative swaddling bands of pink ribbon and lace and made even more effective by bands of metal flower spangles, whose colour is still rich and untarnished, as the doll was always protected by the box. The head is encircled by a halo of matching spangles. Probably German in origin.

£100 – £125

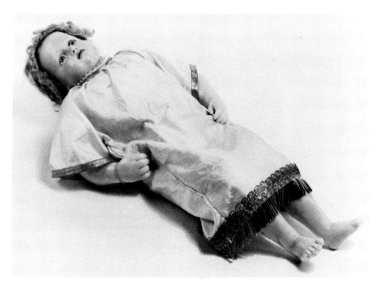

Crib figure
Unmarked. 19th century. Height 53cm:21in.

A poured wax figure of the Infant Jesus, intended for display in a crib
or manger. The head, which is turned to one side for realism, has fixed
blue glass eyes of an unpleasant colour which spoils the effectiveness of
the modelling. It has an attached wig of fair hair and the lips are slightly
parted to reveal the teeth. The body is built up over a wire armature so
that it could be bent into any necessary position in a crib. The silk and
braid decorated costume is original but not very well made. The
modelling of the wax limbs is far superior to that of the head, which is
lacking in detail for its size. Such figures are very much a minority taste
and can be bought quite cheaply.

£30 – £40

Church related figures
Unmarked. 18th century. Height 46cm:18in.

A pair of very effectively constructed Italian crèche figures with terra cotta heads modelled to represent bystanders in a large crèche setting. The woman's head is particularly fine: the mouth is slightly open and the hair finely described and painted with decorative blue ribbons. Both the characters wear the original costumes which are in fine general condition, that of the woman being decorated with originally expensive gold lace. The well-made stands are a great advantage to a collector.

£50 – £75 the pair

Author's collection
A group of shoulder-headed white bisque or parian dolls, except the man who is a blonde bisque. The blonde haired doll, with well moulded hair, wears its original velvet and jet trimmed lilac silk dress. Although the modelling of the man is not particularly fine, it is of interest as few of this larger size are found. The blonde lady is a commoner type of mould but has appeal as the hairstyle is complex. The pale doll in the original costume (c.1865) is the most unusual as it has a beautifully made wig. The girl in the foreground is of the later type. *Prices, left to right: Lady £250, Man £170, Lady £120, Lady with wig £250, Girl £60.*

WOODEN DOLLS

The wooden doll ranges in quality from the craftsman-carved Pandoras of the eighteenth century, to simple stumps, whittled into shape by some early American settler. The so-called Queen Annes continued to be produced until the late 1820s, those of later construction usually having blue glass eyes with pupils, though there are several exceptions. The eighteenth century woodens are always popular with collectors as they are the first really early dolls made in sufficient numbers to appear quite regularly in sales. They are, however, one of the few types of doll whose comparative price has dropped a little, simply because a large number have appeared on the market over a fairly short period. They are obviously of limited supply and must provide a long term sound investment. Very small Baby House dolls of this type are very hard to find, and consequently their price has remained fairly constant.

In the early nineteenth century, large numbers of the wooden dolls with carved combs in their hair, usually referred to as Grödnertals, from their place of origin, were sold extensively in England and Europe. They vary in size from half an inch to about 45 inches and also vary greatly in the amount of detail they were accorded. This is another doll that is popular, as examples are so unmistakably of the Regency period; once again those in the smaller sizes maintain a good comparative price as they fit well into early dolls' houses. Very rare examples might have a waist joint or a swivel neck and the very large sizes are always extremely difficult to find.

The slim elegance of the Grödnertals had given way, by the mid-nineteenth century, to much sturdier wooden dolls but these are not of very great interest, as their quality is not high and they were made over a very long period, some even being made today. Occasionally an example with a superior finish or an interesting expression occurs and will then sell for well above the general price trend. Large numbers of folk type wooden dolls were also made; their standard is not usually high and as they sell, in most cases, for very little, no attempt can be made to lay any price guide line.

It was the American manufacturers who created the finest wooden dolls at the end of the nineteenth century. Firms such as The Vermont Novelty Works produced well-articulated figures that are now highly popular among American collectors but, obviously, rarely seen in Europe. In the early twentieth century another strongly made doll with good articulation was made by the Schoenhut company. Unfortunately the heads often suffered disfiguring damage and examples in really fine condition, considering the large numbers that were made, are the only ones worthy of collectors' serious interest.

Courtesy Christie's South Kensington

Wooden
Unmarked. Probably late 17th century.
Height 43cm:17in.

Carved and painted wooden figures of similar construction to this are seen in the arms of children in very early prints and paintings. The skirts are of a conical construction and the round wooden bases are attached to the waist section by laths. The skirts were then made of stretched canvas. The torsos were carved. In this case the original arms are lost and the huge hands are somewhat unfortunate replacements. The hair is painted and drawn to the back. Originally a wig would have been worn over this. The ears are well carved. Down the cheeks tears are modelled indicating that in all probability this figure was intended to represent some religious character, but it is included in this section as similar doll figures were also made and it indicates the construction of wooden dolls of this early period. The figure would of course be costumed.

£200

Wooden
Unmarked. c.1740. Height 21cm: 8¼in.

Although eighteenth century Baby Houses have sometimes survived,
they have usually lost most of their inhabitants; consequently the price
of this rather mediocre doll is helped considerably by its small size. The
eyes are painted and are given irises, while the blonde wig is tied at the
nape of the neck. The costume consists of a silk petticoat and apron, a
red and white printed jacket, a stomacher and a cape of yellow silk. The
hat is of pink silk.

£250 – £300

Wooden
Unmarked. c.1775. Height 53cm:21in.

The poorly made modern costume ruins the effect of this fine quality eighteenth century English wooden doll with its well-shaped face and widely spaced features. The condition of the head is good and the remains of the original fair wig can be seen. The fork-like wooden hands have some damage and the wooden jointed legs are well-made replacements. Damage to the legs of such early dolls is not as seriously considered as in later woodens and if well repaired does not detract over-much from the price.

£400 – £450

Wooden
Unmarked. 18th century. Height 35cm:14in.

Despite its early date, this doll can only be valued as a fragment of the fine specimen that it once was. It nevertheless holds very considerable primitive charm, as the beech has developed a rich warm patina and the original stitched corset adds to the appeal. Had this doll been complete, it would have been a most interesting specimen as the head has much more characterisation than is usually found on wooden dolls of this period and the huge bulbous eyes are also of much above average quality. Only on the best of eighteenth century dolls were the ears also carved. This is a very interesting specimen from the historical standpoint but of problematical commercial value.

£100 – £120

Courtesy Phillips

Wooden
Unmarked. c.1775. Height 46cm:12¼in.

A pair of fine eighteenth century wooden dolls with large eyes and well-defined and carved features made up as shellcraft ornaments, probably in the early nineteenth century. Unfortunately the original bodies were altered to create the group, so that their potential value is much decreased. The applied shell decoration is enlivened with pieces of mica which give a glittering effect. The figures were displayed in the original silk lined case. The very obvious quality of the heads would have an immediate appeal to any wooden doll enthusiast and the shortcomings of the presentation might be disregarded, though the reselling of such figures might present some difficulty.

£350

Wooden
Unmarked. Mid-18th century. Height 42cm: 16½in.

A good eighteenth century wooden doll probably of English manufacture with a turned wooden body. The lower arms, which are damaged, are wooden and the upper, which are nailed to the torso, are made of fabric. The legs are of the usual jointed type. The head is in good original condition and has the usual dark iris-less eyes. The lambswool wig is nailed in place. The underwear, which is concealed by the reconstructed dress, is particularly fine, especially the quilted petticoat. The effect of the doll is colourful because of the satin embroidered dress trimmed with green fringe but the doll, without these later clothes, is a fairly basic example of the type, though the head is in nice condition.

£450 – £500

Wooden
Unmarked. c.1780. Height 36cm:14in.

Eighteenth century wooden dolls suffer from surges of popularity followed by relative declines and 1977 prices were low compared with those of five or six years previously. This doll is typical of the basic form of the period with its turned wooden body and gessoed and painted head. The eyes are attractive as they are so large and elongated. The original costume consists of a flower printed open robe over a sprigged brown striped petticoat with a yellow silk fichu. A hanging pocket is most finely made but concealed under the robe. An attractive mob cap is worn. The hands are of the fork type with a few fingers missing.

£200 – £250

Wooden
Unmarked. Late 18th century. Height 39cm:15½in.

A fairly good basic Queen Anne type doll, whose appearance is spoiled by the patterned cotton dress of a later date. The eyes are of the dark type and the white painted body has hoof type feet. The arms are of leather. Re-dressed, this is potentially a pleasing doll.

£350 – £400

Courtesy Phillips

Wooden
Unmarked. 18th century Height 33cm: 13in.

A turned and carved doll in poor condition, but it would be possible to restore it to an acceptable standard, as the head only shows the typical wear that would be found on the majority of dolls of this period. The eyes are of the usual iris-less form and the lower part of the nose shows a gouged out chisel mark, indicating the speed with which dolls of this type were constructed by the craftsmen. The top of the head shows the remains of the nails with which the original hair wig would have been fixed to the head. Both the original arms and legs are missing, though the fabric replacements are not recent. The costume is modern.

As the number of dolls surviving from the eighteenth century is fairly limited, even very damaged pieces such as this have some value as, despite its somewhat decrepit state, it would provide a collector with an example of the type.

£125

Wooden
Unmarked. c.1810. Height 64cm:25in.

Early nineteenth century wooden dolls are often characterised by features that appear to be rather 'bunched together' as in this example. The very high pigeon chest is also an indication of a late, though not necessarily nineteenth century, date. Damage to the paint of dolls of this early date does not as radically affect price, as in later figures, as they were easily damaged by damp which caused the gesso to flake away. This doll, with its nicely pointed chin, has tremendous appeal and wears a contemporary quilted saxe blue bonnet. The arms of pink leather are possibly replacements and the wooden legs are jointed. The remains of the hair wig are nailed in position. The striped pink and white cotton frock is some years later than the doll and dates to around 1830.

£350

Courtesy Christie's South Kensington

Wooden
Unmarked. 1805-1820. Height 43cm:17in.

Grödnertals in the larger sizes are only occasionally found and invariably command respectable prices. This doll has the typical carved yellow comb, and the delicately painted black curls to the temples. The eyes are painted brown and the ears are drilled for wire loops for bead earrings. The well made body is jointed at knee, thigh, shoulder and elbow. The shoes are painted red but one foot front is missing. The general condition of the face is a little worrying as the paint is flaking away and small cracks are developing, so that some restoration is necessary in order to avoid further deterioration. The remains of the original costume is worn. Despite the need for restoration, this doll is an elegant example and attractive to the majority of collectors.

£300

Wooden
Unmarked. c.1815-1820. Height 27cm:10½in.

A Grödnertal with the typical wooden body assembled as an ornamental shell figure and consequently losing much of its value as a doll, collectors preferring more conventionally dressed woodens. The ears are given screwed in earrings and the curls at the front are well painted, though there is some unfortunate flaking away of the paint around the neck and on the arms. The skirt is made of a cardboard cone that is lightly cemented with an assortment of shells and the base is seaweed covered. Quite an attractive figure and very typical of the period when ladies enjoyed such minor craft work.

£125

Wooden
Unmarked. c.1820. Height 66cm:26in.

A turned and carved wooden doll of great charm because of the appealing original costume. The blue eyes with dark pupils are of the type usually associated with the early nineteenth century. The head is in good original condition, with characteristic highly coloured pink cheeks and well painted brows. The original blonde wool wig is backed with flannel. The jointed wooden body has white painted legs and kid arms with separately sewn fingers. The doll wears its original pink and white striped dress that once belonged to Lady Anna Gore Langton, only daughter of the 2nd Duke of Buckingham, born in 1821. The fine silk bonnet is trimmed with pink ribbon and lace; the blue slippers and knitted stockings are original.

£500 – £550

Wooden
Unmarked. c.1820. Height 30cm:12in.

It is becoming increasingly difficult to find pedlar dolls in fine original condition and with their full variety of wares displayed intact beneath the original glass shade. The majority carry a large percentage of drapery type items, such as socks and scarves, that were made without too much difficulty but this doll also has a good assortment of such items as saws and woodworking tools as well as baskets, face screens and graters. In addition to the generous variety of wares, the doll itself is of interest as it is a Grödnertal in a good state of preservation. The flower sprigged dress is original as is the cape and hat.

A fine period piece such as this should command a good price as its interest is to general collectors of antiques as well as doll collectors.

£375

Wooden
Unmarked. c.1825. Height 15 and 18cm: 5¾ and 7in.

A pair of very effectively dressed Grödnertals with the usual type of jointed wooden bodies and with red painted slippers. The taller doll has a yellow comb surmounted by a coronet with fringed streamers, while the smaller wears a white silk dress with a train and veil decorated with sequins. The taller doll is of better quality as there is more detail to the face and the hair lying on the cheeks is painted more effectively. Both would provide very fine inhabitants for a dolls' house of the period.

£200 the pair

Courtesy Sotheby's

Wooden
Unmarked. c.1830. Height 21 cm: 8½in.

One of a matched pair of pedlar figures, each in a separate glazed case. The woman wears a label reading 'Amy Scrap Licenced Hawker No. 5367' and the matching man's label reads 'Mark Thrift Licenced Hawker No. 7298'. Each carries a wicker basket of wares. Both the costumes worn and the articles for sale are preserved in beautiful condition.

The Grödnertal wooden dolls from which the pedlars were constructed are attractive dolls in their own right and the man, with painted sideburns, is particularly effective.

£650 the pair

Wooden
Unmarked. c.1830. Height 7.5cm:3in.

A doll of the Grödnertal type that appears immediately saleable because of the charming presentation in a Victorian printed coloured box that once held chocolates. The doll wears its original 1830s style costume with large sleeves of net. The dress has a striped skirt and a pale mauve top. The figure is assembled as a penwiper and on a fan is written 'Present me to wipe your pen'.

£55

Wooden
Unmarked. c.1830. Height 15cm:6in.

The subject of the Old Woman Who Lived in a Shoe with her horde of children is one that has long fascinated dollmakers. In this example, the shoe is probably home-made of pink silk, with pins holding the ribbon around the sole in place. In the shoe is the old woman, a nice quality Grödnertal with good brush strokes to the temples, and six small dolls of the same type, one being carried on her back. All the 'children' are dressed in white cotton but the old woman wears a printed flowered dress and carries a stick for chastisement.

£300

Wooden
Unmarked. 1840s. Height 2.5cm:1in.

A charming group of Grödnertal type jointed dolls still in their original box that carries a label reading 'For dear little Rose with Aunt Emily's love, 1846'. All these minute dolls wear the original costumes in pink, blue and *eau de nil,* and have carved yellow combs in their hair. A great deal of the value would obviously depend upon the chance of the three having been preserved together with their message and date.

£165

Wooden
Unmarked. c.1860. Height 8cm: 3¼in.

The theme of the Old Woman Who Lived In A Shoe is one that has attracted adults of many generations and they have utilised contemporary dolls in their home-made groups. In this version the slipper of faded purple silk is especially made for the purpose and decorated with a yellow bow. The jointed penny woodens and the old woman are chosen to be well in scale and an attractive appearance is achieved. These wooden dolls are of the round faced type that became common from around 1850 and the group is therefore much less desirable than one assembled from the earlier Grödnertals. The costumes of the dolls are also extremely plain, though the whole effect is sufficiently detailed to make this a nice acquisition.

£250 – £260

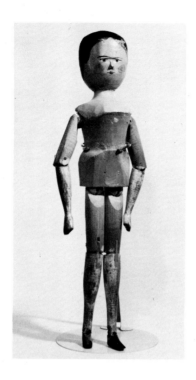

Wooden
Unmarked. c.1845-1850. Height 43cm:17in.

A very well shaped carved wooden doll of the 'wooden top' type with realistically described feet and spoon-like hands indicating an early date. The head is also well painted and in good original condition. Though these dolls were produced in vast quantities in regions such as St. Ulrich and the Swiss Alps, larger examples of this early date have survived only in limited numbers, for they were discarded once damaged because of their low initial cost, whereas a more expensive doll of the same period might have been repaired.

£65 – £75

Wooden
Unmarked. c.1840. Height 42cm:16½in.

A wooden top dating to the middle years of the century but costumed in the style of the 1830s. There is some repair to the figure and the hands appear to be replacements; the lower legs are also too roughly carved to have passed the inspection of the St. Ulrich merchants where the majority of such dolls were assembled for exporting all over Europe. The original costume is charming and consists of a red and white printed apron and a well made black bonnet. A basket of knitting is carried.

£85

Wooden
Unmarked. c.1870. Height 46cm:18in.

The later types of wooden doll are not usually of great interest to collectors, as their round heads are of an almost uniform construction and a single example is usually all that is required. This doll, although the body is of the basic wooden type, has an unusually expressive narrow face that greatly adds to its interest. The eyes are painted blue and the wig is glued in place. Some parts of the costume are original while others are replacements.

Dolls such as these were made in vast numbers in the Swiss and German Alps and exported to England and other European countries in some quantity. The smaller sizes are often found in dolls' houses.

£65

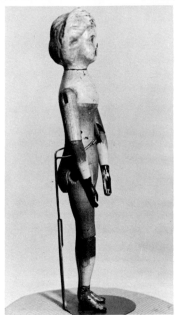

Courtesy Shirley Shalles, Broomall, Pa.

Wooden
Unmarked. c.1873-1874. Height about 38cm:15in.

Three views of a Joel Ellis wooden doll, showing the cleverly constructed joints. Joel Addison Hartley Ellis of Springfield, Vermont, is of great importance in the development of the American doll industry as he made the first commercial wooden doll in that country. The heads, of green rock maple, were steamed until soft and then pressed into shape by machine, while the limbs were lathe-turned. An 1882 advertisement claimed that the "joints can be so manipulated as to place the doll in almost any position". The firm had, by this time, been apparently taken over by George W. Sanders who had registered an improved joint in 1880. The Joel Ellis dolls were strengthened by the addition of metal hands and feet and this example is believed to be the type made by Ellis when president of the Co-operative Manufacturing Company. The dolls are believed to have been made at The Vermont Novelty Works. It is very difficult to attempt to distinguish the dolls made in this area and they are sometimes grouped together and simply described as 'Springfield type'. The heads are often very chipped and are sometimes distressingly repainted but this example is in very nice original condition. Examples are extremely rare in Europe.

£350 – £450

Courtesy Beatrice L. Wright, Phoenixville, Pa.

Wooden
Marked. c.1911-1930. Height approx. 41cm:16in.

Albert Schoenhut, a German immigrant to America, established his own toy factory in 1872 and was granted a patent for spring jointed dolls in 1911. The dolls were very cleverly jointed by wire springs, so that when the feet were pegged in position on the stands that were supplied the dolls could be placed in a variety of poses. They were known as 'All-Wood Perfection Art Dolls' and were supplied with either moulded hair or mohair wigs. The heads were shaped by pressure moulding. In 1924 a cheaper type of elastic jointing was introduced. This wigged example of the earlier type wears its original costume and has painted eyes. The head is in very fine condition and is classed as a 'pouty' type. The Schoenhuts are not as highly regarded in Europe as in the States and sometimes fetch disappointingly low prices at auction.

£100 – £125

Wooden
Unmarked. c.1900. Height 30cm:12in.

A wooden top of the type that continued to be made well into the twentieth century, with a very simply carved body with crudely shaped hands and feet. This example has the advantage of nicely painted hair on the forehead. It is costumed in an old purple frock and re-made underwear.

£18 – £25

Courtesy Phillips

Wooden
Unmarked. 20th century. Height 76cm:30in.

Dolls of the Queen Anne type were collected even in the early twentieth century and reproductions were made, including those in the Victoria and Albert Museum known to English collectors as the 'School for Scandal' dolls, as they were especially made, with no intention of deception, for an exhibition. Despite their known provenance, the V&A dolls are often seen in recently produced books on dolls, described as eighteenth century! This example is a very obvious reproduction with modern blue glass eyes, poorly carved hands, badly jointed legs and an oddly shaped head, suggesting that the maker had never even handled a genuine doll of the type. It is effectively costumed in early nineteenth century fabric with some eighteenth century braid decoration. Such dolls have no real value to collectors but are sometimes bought cheaply simply as amusing items.

£30 – £40

PAPIER MÂCHÉ AND COMPOSITIONS

The early papier mâchés date from the eighteenth century, but there are so few examples found that it is difficult to value them, except as being well over the top range of the nineteenth century examples. As is the case with many antiques of considerable rarity, the average dealer or collector often avoids an item that he finds difficult to value; consequently early dolls of this type are sometimes sold for comparatively disappointing figures.

The majority of nineteenth century examples are of German origin and closely reflect the shape of women of the period, with their slim, high-waisted bodies and complicated fashionable hairstyles. It is usually by these hairstyles that dolls of this type are dated. When in the original gauze costumes supplied by the manufacturer, the dolls are often rather unexciting in appearance, but fortunately most of the original owners re-dressed them and the clothes are often very finely sewn. The papier mâché heads are very easily damaged by extremes of climate and this damage does influence price (though to nothing like the extent it does in bisques), the damage being mainly caused by ageing.

In the 1840s a much plumper type of doll evolved, whose leather or fabric body was given some movement by means of a gusset at the hip. A simple painted hairstyle was added to the smooth head, which meant that the same basic doll could be dressed either as a man or, by the addition of a wig, as a woman. After 1860, the standard of papier mâchés dropped considerably and they were made to represent children rather than adults. Some of these later dolls, usually referred to by collectors as Compositions, have pretty faces and, if in good condition, càn look very attractive, but much of their value depends on the originality and effectiveness of the costume. Simple types of papier mâchés continued to be produced until the late 1920s, though dolls as late as this are of interest at present mainly as curiosities rather than collectors' items.

The price of the early 19th century papier mâchés rose steeply around 1974, collectors suddenly seeming to become aware of their appeal but, as is often the case with a sudden steep rise, prices since this time have remained fairly static, which means a drop in real terms. Due to the excellent prices being obtained in the salerooms, many collectors, who were, perhaps, not overfond of their papier mâchés, decided to realise their investment and this caused a temporary flooding of the market, though this seemed to be slowing down by 1977.

Papier Mâché
Unmarked. 1735-1740. Height 63.5cm:25in.

Eighteenth century papier mâchés are characterised by their full and rather flat faces but examples are extremely rare, especially those wearing original dress in as good a condition as this. The papier mâché head has inset blue glass eyes and a brown hair wig. The jointed wooden legs have metal hooks at the thigh and knee which keep the legs straight when the doll is in a standing position. The hands are of carved wood and have a fork shape associated with the eighteenth century woodens. The general condition of the head is very good, though few would consider it really beautiful. The original costume comprised two shifts, a circular ticking hoop, knitted green silk stockings and shoes in silver and green brocade. The pink, lace trimmed bodice fastens at the front with green ribbon and the elaborate sack-backed mantua in striped coral, green and white silk has a full train. A matching petticoat is worn. The doll is therefore a fascinating costume document as well as a good basic collector's piece.

£600 – £700

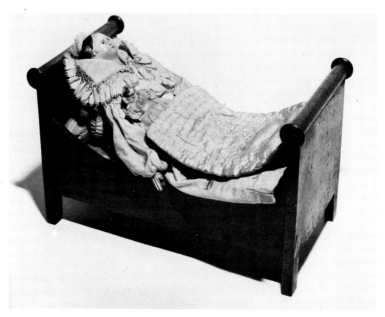

Papier Mâché
Unmarked. c.1820. Length 20cm:8in.

A well made early nineteenth century bed in which lie a mother and child. The 'baby' is a basic Grödnertal but the mother is more interesting as she has brown hair swept into a bun and a fabric body with wooden lower arms. The lower parts of the legs, which should be of wood, are unfortunately missing. The original well made nightgown is worn and the quilt and bolsters on the bed are also effectively made.

£100 − £120

Courtesy Phillips

Papier Mâché
Unmarked. c.1830. Height 41cm:16in.

A doll with a most effective general appearance because of its lavish costume of green silk and lace ornamented with beads, with chains and medallions worn around the neck, representing a Bavarian woman in wedding dress. The head is of the basic early nineteenth century papier mâché type with painted blue eyes and black painted coiffure type hair. Over this, a very fine and ornate wig is applied that contributes greatly to the detailed effect. The head has a very bad crack on one side and is mounted on a very poor body with badly carved hands, not of the standard that would be associated with the wooden bodies made at the time in Germany and probably a late nineteenth century replacement because of damage. If a more appropriate body could be found, this is potentially a most interesting doll as the costume is still restorable.

£150 − £175

Papier Mâché
Unmarked. c. 1835. Height 19cm:7½in.

A papier mâché headed lady doll with a kid body and wooden limbs, the joins neatened with blue paper bands. The black hair is moulded with coils over the ears and drawn into a pointed knot at the back. The eyes are painted in blue. Though papier mâchés usually have a very strong period feel, this example, for some reason, is completely unevocative, the whole figure having a very mean appearance.

£100 – £110

Papier mâché
Unmarked. c.1835. Height 30.5cm:12in.

A papier mâché with the moulded hair swept into a plaited bun at the back of the head and looped forward at the front to reveal the ears. This showing of the ears on either a papier mâché or a porcelain head is always liked by collectors. The body is of the usual construction for the type with wooden lower arms and legs and sawdust-filled leather torso. Flat heeled slippers are painted green and neatening bands are red. The effect of the figure is enhanced by the original silk dress with a petticoat and chemise and a short fringed velvet cape. The effectively made original bonnet is carried to reveal the detail of the head and hair.

£400

Courtesy Author

Courtesy Sotheby's

Courtesy Phillips

Papier Mâché
Unmarked. c.1830. Diameter 24cm:9½in.

A small wooden bodied figure, with the head made of a type of composition which has now a slightly crumbling appearance and a dark hair wig. A large satin hat is worn. It lies in a very charming and delicately coloured setting of flowers and rosettes which contributes most effectively to the fragility of the doll. The lidded box is covered with printed paper. The whole setting was probably intended as a Valentine but is highly collectable as so completely original and so well presented.

£250 – £275

Papier Mâché
Unmarked. c.1835. Height 34cm:13½in.

The modelling of papier mâché heads became much more simple as the century progressed and by 1835 the very ornately moulded coiffure type heads had gone out of fashion, though still occasionally made into the 1840s. They were succeeded by bald-headed shoulder heads with the very simple hairstyle painted in dark brown or black. A slit was sometimes cut along the crown and hair pushed through and arranged around the face as in the more common waxed composition slit heads. The wooden arms and legs were also dispensed with and the whole body made of fine leather with, quite often, gussets to the buttocks. It was once thought, mainly because of a comment made by d'Allemagne, that the bodies were made in France and the heads in Germany, and though this might occasionally have been true, I now consider that the majority are purely of German origin. Papier mâchés are also recorded as having been made in England, but it is at present impossible to attribute any examples directly to this country and collectors generally now assume a German origin. This doll wears its original pink trimmed straw bonnet, a black lace trimmed shawl and a red and brown patterned woollen dress. A charming correctly made parasol with a bone handle is carried.

£225

Papier Mâché
Unmarked. c.1835-1840. Height 33cm:13in.

A woman pedlar doll with a papier mâché head and painted features wearing the original green worsted skirt, printed brown cotton jacket and apron, a checked shawl and a black bonnet. She is standing at a market stall that is lavishly stocked with crabs, fish, baskets of seashells, birds, fish and vegetables, the whole protected by a glass shade. An almost identical pedlar figure is to be seen at the Tunbridge Wells Museum, again indicating how many of the figures that were once considered individually made at home are in fact commercial.

Pedlar doll prices tend to swing quite suddenly, so that at the time of writing (1977) some dolls have fetched almost ludicrously low prices while others, such as this example, went surprisingly high. The general trend is therefore here indicated in the suggested price.

£500 – £600

Papier Mâché
Unmarked. c.1840. Height 44.5cm:17½in.

Dolls as rare as this example only occasionally appear in the salerooms and it is almost impossible to predict what the price realised might be. These figures with skirts that conceal a kitchen are peculiarly of German origin and similarly constructed monks are seen in old catalogues. The doll's metal foot, which can be seen at the front of the base, acts as a catch for the door. The interior is in original condition with various letters and numbers, written in ink, suggesting where items should be hung. When the doors are closed, the effect of a skirt is given. The composition doll is costumed in brown silk, damaged probably past the point of repair, and a straw bonnet. The contents of the original doll are largely missing and have been added to with much more recent brass and china. With some time spent in collecting correct period items for the kitchen this doll could again be a real collector's treasure.

£600 – £700

Papier Mâché
Unmarked. 1840-1850. Height 37cm and 28cm:14½in. and 11in.

The larger doll has moulded centre-parted hair that is drawn into a braided coil at the back. The shoulder head is in reasonable condition and only has a few very fine cracks. The lower parts of both the arms and legs are made of wood and the body is of fabric rather than the leather that is more generally preferred by collectors. A contemporary quilted pink petticoat is worn with a flower printed blue chintz open robe and a black silk cape and bonnet making an effective costume.

The smaller doll carrying knitting and a can is of similar construction, but has a slightly different hair style. A purple and black cotton dress is worn with a scarlet apron and a black bonnet.

Larger doll, £400 – £450
Small, £250 – £280

Papier Mâché
Unmarked. c.1840. Height 38cm:15in.

Papier mâchés with their hair arranged in long ringlets such as this are frequently rather shallow in definition, but this example has extremely well modelled hair. Basically this example is a head and shoulders on a body that was probably repaired or remade some hundred years ago. The dolls of this type left the manufacturers with wooden lower arms and lower legs and buyers are not usually happy with a head of this type mounted on a completely fabric body. It is possible that some papier mâché heads were sold for home assembly, but this doll is certainly very much in need of restoration.

The black painted hair is plaited into a bun at the back and the eyes are painted blue. It is dressed in the original net frock.

£250 – £275

Papier Mâché
Unmarked. c.1840. Height 53cm:21in.

This rather plump type of papier mâché doll is particularly associated with the 1840s, when the tall elegant type of papier mâché was going out of fashion. The pale coloured and lightly varnished head has black iris-less eyes of glass and the lips are slightly parted to reveal teeth of bamboo. The hair is painted but the original wig is attached over this. The sawdust filled leather body is gusseted for articulation and has separately stitched fingers. The doll wears the original costume of printed flowered cotton, with a pink silk bonnet trimmed with black velvet, lace and flowers. Though not generally considered beautiful dolls, these transitional papier mâchés are of interest in the development of the medium and most serious collectors like to own an example.

£350

Courtesy Phillips

Papier Mâché
Unmarked. c.1845. Height 51cm:20in.

A Sonneberg type papier mâché with an open mouth and inset bamboo teeth showing how a more child-like doll was gradually evolving. The hair wig is loosely plaited and the fixed glass eyes are of the dark iris-less type. The shoulder head is mounted on a stuffed fabric body with rather out-of-scale lower arms made of composition. The legs are slightly strange and of a pale cream colour, modelled very high and possibly old replacements. Black leather shoes are worn and a striped mauve, white and red dress.

£150 – £175

Courtesy Beatrice L. Wright, Phoenixville, Pa.

Papier Mâché
Marked with label on shoulder. 1858 label. Height 61cm:24in.

The Greiner dolls are a landmark in the development of the native American doll, as this firm registered the first known patent for a head. The 1858 patent specification described a mixture of 1 lb of white paper, 1 lb Spanish whiteing, 1 lb rye flour, 1oz glue together with linen that was used to reinforce the more fragile parts of the head. The 1858 version is usually found with black hair and this example is moulded in a particularly crisp and attractive style. It is mounted on a cloth body. The label on the shoulder reads 'Greiners Patent Doll Head. Pat. March 30 1858'. As these dolls were made for the home market they are rarely found in Europe, though most collectors would like to own an example.

£400 – £450

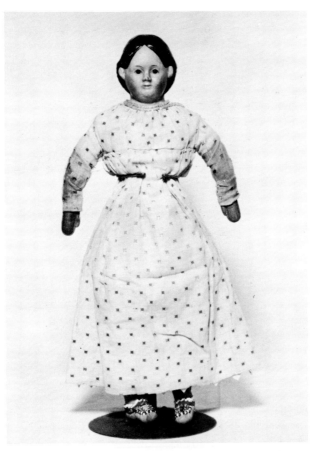

Courtesy Beatrice L. Wright, Phoenixville, Pa.

Papier Mâché
Marked with label. 1858 label. Height 46cm:18in.

This American doll is another example of the work of Ludwig Greiner. The original 1858 patent was extended in 1872 and dolls made to the later specification include as many fair as dark haired heads. The majority have painted eyes. This example with the early label, has hair moulded in a much simpler style and painted eyes. It wears an original cotton dress and is mounted on a cloth body.

£350 − £375

Courtesy Phillips

Composition
Unmarked. c.1875. Height 37cm:14½in.

This is basically a fairly cheap composition, but is made attractive by the original effectively made blue silk dress which dates the figure. The composition head is of the full domed type with fixed blue glass eyes and a mohair wig. The shoulder head fits the fabric body with composition lower arms and lower legs. The moulded boots are painted blue and decorated with painted white buttons and red tassels. The complete figure illustrates how a very cheap doll becomes an object of collectable interest because of good costume.

£100 – £120

Composition
Unmarked. c.1875. Height 58cm:23in.

A German composition doll with fixed blue glass eyes and the original mohair wig. Compositions of this type are rarely marked and it is probable that some were also made in England. It is mounted on the wrong body but with original arms. The lower body is of the slit headed type and there is a bad crack to the shoulder. The white cotton dress is original.

£35 – £50

Composition
Unmarked. c.1880. Height 61cm:24in.

A very basic composition child doll made very striking because of the well made costume. The head is in fair condition, though there is some cracking around the eyes, but the colour is still fresh and the light varnish undisturbed. Often attempts were made to clean such heads, with the result that the delicate varnish was removed and an unpleasant powdery effect resulted. The original mohair wig is worn and the blue glass eyes are fixed. The body is of the basic stuffed type with composition lower parts, the feet being modelled with realistic toes rather than the moulded boots that are so often found on dolls of this cheap type. The Christening robe is hand-embroidered and the bonnet is made with detailed frilling and pleating.

£140 – £150

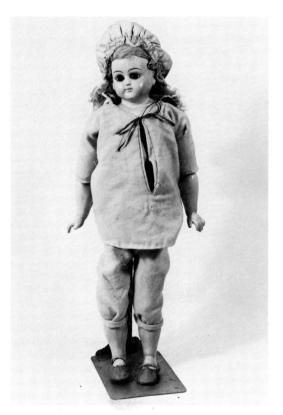

Courtesy Sotheby's

Composition
Marked'A C&O Dressel'. c.1880. Height 48cm:19in.

The engaging cream woollen bathing-suit worn by this doll gives it an immediate appeal, especially as the original hat is still retained and dolls are only occasionally found in any type of sporting clothes. Its main interest, however, lies in the basic construction of the body itself. The top half is quite conventional and consists of a shoulder head mounted on a fabric torso, but from the waist down the complete doll is made of jointed composition. The complete arms are also jointed composition with fixed wrists. The body, costume and shoulder head are all in fine original condition and the head still has its original rather delicate varnish that has all too often worn away in such figures.

£100

Papier Mâché
Unmarked. c.1835-1840. Height 30.5cm:12in.

A wooden bodied pedlar figure in completely original state wearing a printed cotton dress and a woollen cape. The papier mâché head is modelled with unusual delicacy and the face is much longer than is usual on examples of this type. The tray of wares is tipped forward, but when refixed in the correct position a good assortment of home-made wares is shown. These flat basket-edged containers are often found with pedlars and seem to have been especially constructed for the purpose. It is unlikely that this figure was home assembled, as others with identical dresses and wares are known, though they are without the purely commercial effect of those made by White of Milton, Portsmouth.

£300 – £350

Courtesy Phillips

Composition
Unmarked. c.1885. Height 35cm:14in.

A composition girl doll with a wig of abundant auburn hair, but in generally very poor condition. It is of the shoulder headed type but the open mouth has lost all its teeth and the composition is also rubbed. The body is straw-filled with composition lower parts. An old but much too large dress is worn. This doll would only be of interest to a collector with a flair for restoration, as the amount of work involved would not be worth while for a professional dealer.

£15

Composition
Unmarked. c.1880. Height 33cm:13in.

Composition dolls are often spoiled by their over blatant modelling but this doll's face is quite delicately finished with dark painted brows and fixed brown eyes. The lower legs are composition and are modelled with painted black boots and red garters and the lower arms are also composition. The original costume is well made and highly effective and represents a woman in Siberian bridal costume. Though figures in national costumes are not too highly regarded by doll buyers the value of this doll is enhanced by its dress as it is so intricately constructed.

£80 – £85

Courtesy Antiques of Childhood, Camden Passage

Papier Mâché
Marked 'M&S'. c.1920. Height 53cm:21in.

Composition or debased papier mâché dolls of this late period are often found with a very small and narrow shoulder plate, as in this example, with legs that are modelled to well above the knee to allow for the shorter clothes children were wearing. The body is fabric and contains a voice box and the head is appealing, as the brown eyes are painted with some expression. The impressed M&S mark is at present unidentifiable. The doll wears a green velvet suit. The figure is of interest, as the papier mâché is so thin, whereas at this time most of the dollmakers were turning to a much heavier type that was suitable for the much rougher play of the early twentieth century.

£20 – £25

Courtesy Phillips

Reproduction Doll
Unmarked. Modern. Height 32cm:12½in.

Many of these rather crudely made resin dolls have appeared in the antique markets during the last year, being described as 'old'. The surface is treated to resemble some sort of wood or composition but the modelling of the face has nothing of the antique. It has glass eyes and a mohair wig. This example is dressed in the remains of an Edwardian hand towel. It does seem a pity that the makers of such dolls do not mark them clearly, as objects that are originally sold with no attempt to deceive are often later misrepresented by the unscrupulous or ignorant and are a trap for beginner collectors.

£3

WAX DOLLS

Dolls made of wax have a very long history but those that the collector is likely to find date from the eighteenth and nineteenth centuries. Examples found in the eighteenth century Baby Houses are usually modelled from solid wax, with additional detail carved on the surface, such as those made with great skill and found in the Dutch cabinet houses. Two basic types of wax doll were made, those of poured wax, which were always expensive, because of the amount of hand finishing required, and those made of composition shells that were wax-dipped, a process used for cheaper dolls.

Occasionally, waxed compositions dating from the eighteenth century appear at sales; their main interest, however, lies in their costume, as the basic dolls are almost identical to those of the early nineteenth century. Waxed compositions were made both in England and Germany as well as France and America, but it is extremely difficult to decide on the country of origin unless the original costume is intact. This type of doll continued to be produced until the 1920s, though by this time only the cheapest types were sold. Examples tend to swing widely in price, depending on which countries are the strong doll buyers at a particular time. The continental dealers appreciate a look of antiquity and buy for comparatively high prices, whereas the Americans and Japanese find dolls too easily affected by extremes of climate and often rather ugly for a display collection, as, by the nature of the construction, the wax contracts unevenly away from the papier mâché base.

Poured wax dolls have soared in popularity during the last three years, from those that could be bought from specialist dealers for around £70, to exceptional examples now fetching over £300. Again it was originally the German interest that provided a sudden stimulus but the market now seems quite prepared to accept the new level as it continues to rise. The English were the most skilled in the making of poured waxes and any dolls that are marked with names such as Pierotti or Montanari are of greater interest than those whose makers' names can only be speculated upon. Individual factories worked with almost identical methods and were aiming at a doll that resembled a sweet child, so characteristic differences between products are very much in the area of unreliable speculation.

Some damage has usually to be accepted on dolls of this type, as fingers break very easily, and even a fine crack running across a cheek need not lead to the doll being considered of no value. The price an individual example will fetch at auction, if it is unattributable, depends almost entirely on its appeal. Quite well-made examples are sometimes sold relatively cheaply because the face has the 'wrong expression', while another that is late and of poor general construction will fetch a high price because the expression is attractive. The originality of the costume is also of great importance as redressed wax dolls are rarely completely satisfactory. They were originally considered as expensive dolls to be cherished, which is why, despite their fragility, a considerable number have survived.

Courtesy Christie's South Kensington

Waxed Composition
Unmarked. c.1780. Height 45cm:17½in.

A doll of waxed composition with dark iris-less glass eyes and brown wig of human hair. The face has the cracking usually associated with this type of construction. The body is made of linen and filled with sawdust. The arms are of blue kid and are given separately stitched fingers. The main interest of this doll lies in its original costume, which consists of a brown silk open robe with a blue satin petticoat. The stockings are of silk, the remains of the gauze apron can be seen and the gauze hat is trimmed with blue ribbons. Despite the great interest of the costume and the early date for this type of doll, the condition of the doll itself would detract from its desirability in the eyes of many collectors.

£185 – £200

Waxed Composition
Unmarked. c.1810. Height 54cm:21½in.

The value of this fairly basic doll is considerably enhanced by the fact that its history is known. It originally belonged to The Honourable Frances Elizabeth Spencer, 1808-1884, daughter of Lord Francis Spencer, later Lord Churchill. It was then passed through various godchildren to the present owner. It is always difficult to evaluate the importance of pedigree but in this case, whereas the basic doll would be expected to fetch some £175-£200, this example reached £320. It has wired brown eyes and a sawdust-filled linen body. The white kid arms are sewn with five fingers and are in unusually nice condition. The original white cotton frock is worn with silk stockings, blue kid shoes and net cap. The additional garments include a nightgown, sunbonnet, pinafore, cape and petticoat. It is contained in a well-made and lined oak box.

£250

Waxed Composition
Unmarked. c.1815. Height 48cm:19in.

A completely charming Regency waxed composition wearing the original blue silk and lace costume with matching blue leather arms. The eyes are of a particularly brilliant blue with black pupils. The original fair wig, set in curls, is made on a muslin base. The body is of the basic sawdust-filled type and original cream leather front-laced boots are retained, though a little strange with evening dress. Though this doll is of a fairly basic type, it would be a good addition to any collection as it is so engagingly original.

£165

Waxed Composition
Unmarked. 1835-1840. Height 49cm:19½in.

The sudden swings in the prices of dolls can hardly be better illustrated than by waxed compositions of this type, which have moved from the position of being virtually unsaleable for more than £25-£30 some years ago to fetching as much as £200 in 1977. Much of the doll trade relied until that time on the American market, that has little affection for wax, but now that the German and Dutch collectors are active these dolls have swung into saleroom popularity, though provincial dealers still find them difficult to sell. The doll in the boldly patterned frock has sleeping blue eyes, moved by a wire from the waist. The cloth body has the usual leather arms. The other doll, of the same construction, wears a green and white striped frock with red morocco slippers and a straw hat.

£400 the pair

Waxed Composition
Unmarked. c.1835-1840. Height 38cm:15in.

A waxed composition slit-headed doll with very strange protuberant blue glass eyes. The head, with its original wig, shows the distressing common to the type. The body is of sawdust-filled fabric but the original leather lower arms are missing and it now has fabric-wrapped wire stumps. The original Welsh style costume is worn with a tall beaver hat, and a basket of knitting is carried. A frozen Charlotte is nursed under the other arm. The missing arms are an obvious disadvantage but the general effect of the group is pleasing.

£150 – £175

Waxed Composition
Unmarked. c.1840. Height 51cm:20in.

A waxed composition girl with dark brown iris-less eyes and dark hair, arranged in ringlets and inserted into a slit in the head. The sawdust-filled body has pink kid arms. The original brown challis frock trimmed with blue braid is worn. The majority of these dolls were once thought to have originated in Germany but evidence would now suggest that many were of English manufacture. They are found in very large numbers in England but now only occasionally in Germany.

£180 − £190

Waxed Composition
Unmarked. c.1840. Height 68cm:27in.

An impressive large waxed composition wearing a contemporary red and white cotton dress trimmed with lace and braid. The eyes are of the iris-less dark type and are wired to open and close. The heavy realistic arms are an indication of the 1840s when a more natural doll began to be made. The wig, in long brown ringlets, is original as is the well-made grey silk bonnet.

£225 – £250

Waxed Composition
Unmarked. c.1840. Height 76cm:30in.

A waxed composition lady doll dressed in the costume of a child and wearing a red woollen embroidered cape. These waxed compositions, that were first made in the eighteenth century, have survived in some number despite the disfiguring cracks that occurred because of radical changes of temperature. The cracks do not affect price as they would in other types of doll but are accepted as a characteristic. It seems that the majority were made in Germany but it is also probable that some were made in England. The eyes in this example are made to open and close by means of a wire lever.

£150

Courtesy Sotheby's

Waxed Composition
Unmarked. Mid 19th century. Height about 43cm:17in.

The general appearance of fairly basic dolls is greatly enhanced when presented in an original glazed case. The desirability is increased for the collector by the fact that two basic types of typically mid-nineteenth century dolls are represented together in a relatively small space and both are well preserved examples of the type. They both wear cream gauze dresses trimmed with blue ribbon, beads and artificial flowers. The smaller doll is a typical yellow haired pumpkin head with wooden lower arms attached to a sawdust-filled muslin body while the other is of the Motschmann type with blue glass eyes and an open mouth revealing the teeth. The Motschmann dolls represent the German makers' attempt to make a more realistic baby type of doll based on the Oriental pattern. They were also made in some number in composition.

£300 – £350

Waxed Composition
Unmarked. c.1859-1860. Height 37cm:14½in.

A waxed composition Motschmann type doll in unusually perfect condition. When a squeaker in the torso is pressed, the head turns and the limbs move. The carton and wire body has waxed composition limbs. The fixed glass eyes are blue and there are delicately painted curls above the ears. The mouth is slightly open to reveal the bamboo teeth.

£150 – £185

Waxed Composition
Unmarked. Mid 19th century. Height 33cm:13in.

A most unusual waxed composition doll that is modelled as a Chinese with slanting dark eyes. Several different Oriental heads were made in the mid-nineteenth century, but this is especially nice as it also has a moulded and painted Chinese hat with four bells suspended from wires on the crown. The body contains a squeaker and, when pressed, this causes the wooden legs and arms to move, clashing the metal cymbals and causing the head to move from side to side. The clothes were once brightly coloured but only the remains are now seen.

£200 – £250

Courtesy Phillips

Waxed Composition
Unmarked. c.1855. Height 72cm:28½in.

A waxed pumpkin head of an impressive size and with the cracking of
the surface common to this type of construction. The fixed eyes are of
the dark iris-less type and the hair, held in position by a moulded black
band, is a typical fair colour. The body is fabric and made without a
voice box. The carved wooden boots are painted blue. The costume was
made up from scraps of contemporary material added, probably
because of damage, to the original red sprigged bodice. The general
effect is, however, quite pleasing as so completely period.

£140 – £160

Waxed Composition
Unmarked. c.1845. Height 69cm:27in.

The collector's term for waxed composition dolls where the hair is set into a channel cut along the centre of the crown is a 'slit head'. This is a particularly good example of the type, as the wax has only cracked very slightly and does not disfigure the head at all. The wire lever that protrudes at the hip effects the movement of the black iris-less eyes, so they can be made to sleep. This mechanism still works well. The wig is also in fine condition, as are the red leather arms. The body is of the typical construction for the type, having turned-in fabric feet and being filled with sawdust. The pale green woollen dress trimmed with lace and braid is authentic and complete underwear composed of drawers, chemise, a calico waist petticoat and a muslin petticoat are worn. The head has been cleaned and the brows probably repainted at some time.

£185 – £200

Courtesy Phillips

Waxed Composition
Unmarked. c.1855. Height 38cm:15in.

A simple German waxed composition with inset black iris-less eyes. The body is of fabric and contains a squeaker voice box. The lower limbs are of wood and the joints at wrist level give the figure a little added interest as one piece wooden lower arms are more usual. Originally the doll would have worn a wig but this is now missing. Such dolls were made in large numbers and originally sold very cheaply so there is rarely any detailed finishing of the basic doll.

The main value of this particular example lies in the very large wardrobe of contemporary clothes that accompany the doll. All the pieces are finely stitched by hand and there are several dresses as well as underwear. Unfortunately such dolls are often bought by dealers or even collectors who divide the wardrobes and use the costumes for other dolls. Historically, this is obviously a sad practice but it accounts for the high price that a very ordinary doll such as this can achieve.

£160 (with wardrobe), £100 without

Courtesy Christie's South Kensington

Waxed Composition
Unmarked. c.1860. Height 25.5cm:10in.

A waxed composition with a stuffed body containing a squeaker. The lower arms are of composition as are the legs that are modelled with spats. Though basically a cheap type of doll, the head is interesting as it is modelled with a guardsman's feather bonnet with a gilt plate and red and white plume. The brown hair is also moulded and painted; the fixed eyes are glass. As so many different types of bonnet heads were made, both in bisque and composition as well as waxes of this type. they form a small collecting field by themselves.

£120

Waxed Composition
Unmarked. c.1860. Height 41cm:16in.

Waxed compositions in the 1850s and 60s were sometimes given wigs made up of small pads of mohair that created an effect very similar to that of the moulded pumpkin heads. This doll wears its original wig and has fixed iris-less eyes. The shoulder head is mounted on a fabric body with composition hands and feet. It was redressed in blue silk and lace, probably in the 1870s, and is now contained in a glazed case.

£100 – £125

Waxed Composition
Unmarked. c.1860. Height 40.5cm:16in.

Waxed composition heads of this type are usually described as 'pumpkin' or 'squash' heads because of the fairly shallow two-piece moulds in which they were made. They were produced from around 1850 until 1865 though variants occasionally appear later. They are generally thought to be of German origin. Value depends very much upon condition and the rarity of the particular mould.

This example, with its short moulded hair held in place by a band, is one of the more common designs and the price is further restrained by the lack of original clothes. The eyes are black and iris-less and the wax shows some disfiguring shrinkage around the eyes. The torso contains a press voice box that no longer works. The lower arms and legs are simply carved of wood. This is a fairly satisfactory example of the type and when costumed should look quite effective.

£120 – £130

Courtesy Christie's South Kensington

Waxed Composition
Marked '2'. c.1870-1875. Height 41cm:16in.

The majority of collectors like to own at least a few late waxed compositions, but examples in really good condition only occasionally appear. The basic doll is fairly ordinary but it is made more desirable by the original costume, consisting of a mauve silk frock and a peplum, both trimmed with lace. The long blonde wig is also original. The limbs are waxed and the modelled feet with toes are not often seen on dolls of the 1870s.

Waxed compositions of this type were made in the greatest quantity in Germany but also in England and France.

£200

Waxed Composition
Unmarked. c.1884. Height 52cm:20½in.

A very wide variety of waxed composition lady dolls was made in the late nineteenth and early twentieth centuries both in Germany and, probably, in England. The quality of the heads is often poor but in this case the wax coating is very heavy and a much more individualistic appearance than usual is achieved. This figure has the added charm of very full documentation having been purchased by Lady Balogh's grandmother, Mrs. Gaselee, c.1884.

The hair is implanted in the wax coating and the head is turned effectively to the right. The fixed eyes are of brown glass. The body is of a much cheaper construction with waxed lower arms and legs.

The main value of this doll and its attractiveness to a collector lies in the excitingly detailed clothes representing fashionable court dress of the period in ivory silk and lace and with a pale gold damask train. The costume is further decorated with ribbons and feathers and a very well made miniature fan is carried.

£250 – £260

Courtesy Phillips

Waxed Composition
Unmarked. c.1885. Height 76cm:30in.

A very large waxed composition with blue fixed eyes and a closed mouth. The original fair mohair wig is worn and the shoulder head has the crazing that is common to dolls of this type. The body is fabric and the lower arms composition. The lower legs are modelled with black shoes. This doll is made attractive by the original costume of blue cotton dress and lace-trimmed bonnet.

£75 – £80

Waxed Composition
Unmarked. c.1875. Height 53cm:21in.

A waxed composition of the cheapest type with very little modelling to the face but of some interest as the original colouring of the features is completely untouched — usually the colouring rubs away. The body is made of straw-filled cotton and the lower arms and legs are composition. The original cream, mauve and green silk frock is worn with a red sash and a muslin pinafore. Though a cheap doll, it is interesting because of its good condition.

£50 – £75

Waxed Composition
Unmarked. c.1885. Height 36cm:14in.

A two-faced waxed composition baby that was probably made by Fritz Bartenstein, who obtained patents for such dolls in 1880 and 1881. This example has brown glass eyes. The howling face has an open mouth showing the tongue, while the smiling face has painted teeth. The voice box, activated, together with the head, by pulling a string at the side of the body, is enclosed in the torso. The lower parts of the limbs are composition. The figure wears its original grey silk and plum velvet dress and bonnet.

The doll is made more interesting as its history is known; it was bought in Paris in 1899 by Lady Sitwell and given to her head gardener's daughter, Alice Louise Williams, who was born in 1889.

£300 – £350

Wax
Unmarked. 18th century. Height 23cm:9in.

Figures similar in construction to this wax headed man, who carries a bird in a cane cage, are found, almost without exception, to be of Dutch origin and were intended as some sort of ornamental item rather than for play. Ladies holding fruit as well as men with simple genre items are found and it would appear that the intention was similar to that of the nineteenth century English makers of pedlar dolls. This figure wears a silk coat and a tall felt hat. The legs are made of wood.

£100

Courtesy Phillips

Wax
Unmarked. c.1780. Height 38cm:15in.

A wax-headed doll originally of fine quality and dating to the eighteenth century with the typical dark blue bead eyes of this period. The ornate wig is made of a substance rather like tow and sewn to a flannel type backing. Some parts of the costume appear original but sections, such as the petticoat, are reconstructed. The value of the doll, potentially of great interest, is much diminished by the very strange body, which is sticky to the touch and distinctly unpleasant in atmosphere. It is unusually heavy and seems to be constructed from a metal armature with some waxen substance wrapped about with fabric. The arms are made of leather and a muff was originally carried. The original black shoes with metal buckles are worn. For some unknown reason this doll is quite distasteful to handle, a feeling that was reflected by the low price it fetched despite its age and potential interest.

£75

Poured Wax
Unmarked. c.1840. Height 10cm:4in.

A small poured wax doll that would make a very suitable inhabitant for a dolls' house of the period. It has the dark, beady eyes associated with the smaller early nineteenth century poured waxes and still wears the original nicely plaited blonde wig. Slippers are painted on the feet. The original blonde and net frock, edged with green silk, is also retained. The whole effect is very charming.

£85 – £100

Poured Wax
Unmarked. Early 19th century. Height 12.5cm:5in.

Poured wax baby dolls dating to the first half of the nineteenth century are not common, and this pair, with plump shoulders and well-turned fairly realistic heads, is particularly effective. The eyes are painted blue rather than the dark bead-like eyes normally associated with this period, and instead of a more usual wig the short brown hair is painted with side partings. They wear the original white nightgowns and bonnets trimmed with pink silk ribbons and are contained in a basket type bed. Though very small in size these are quite rare and of interest to any wax doll enthusiast.

£240 – £300

Poured Wax
Unmarked. c.1835. Height 25.5cm:10in.

An unusual bazaar stall assembled on a circular base and sold with a paper inscribed 'This bazaar made by me in 1835, renovated . . . 1873' and signed E. Mabyn. The wax-headed doll, modelled to resemble an old woman, has a stuffed body and kid arms. It is costumed in faded aubergine satin and wears a muslin cap. The seller stands behind a half circular mahogany table with four turned legs that is hung with contemporary items including a cotton frock, an apron and bonnets. On the table is a cradle, miser's purse, slippers, needle case and sheet music. The group is extremely interesting as it is precisely dated and the maker's name is known.

£500

Poured Wax
Unmarked. Mid 19th century. Height 76cm:30in.

A refreshingly original example of a mid-nineteenth century poured wax doll in its silk dress trimmed with black lace and a dark brown velvet coat with a quilted lining. The extremely effective straw hat trimmed with flowers is also completely authentic. The well stitched underwear consists of drawers, chemise and petticoat; red leather boots with elastic sides are worn. The costume therefore has the double attribute of being both extremely eye catching and original. The basic doll is of the usual poured wax construction but without eyelets. The eyes are blue and the hair inset. The shoulder was broken at some stage and was very badly repaired and the feet also have some damage. Fortunately the damaged areas cannot be seen when the doll is costumed and would not have as much effect on price as when visible.

£250

Courtesy Phillips

Waxed Composition
Unmarked. c.1875. Height 32cm:12½in.

The basic dolls of waxed composition that are contained in this effective room setting are attractive but unexceptional except with regard to their fine state of original preservation. The amusingly created 'room', with a paper mirror and a découpage Christmas tree in the background, makes a most charming period piece and an antique object whose appeal would not be limited to doll collectors. The dolls have blue glass eyes and ruched net dresses. Their waxed boots are typical of those seen, for instance, on marked Dressel dolls. The small hanging lamp is a miniature collector's treasure. The background is created from figures cut from women's fashion magazines of the 1870s. The basic dolls would not be of any great value but the complete group creates a separate value of its own.

£250

Courtesy Sotheby's

Poured Wax
Unmarked. c.1840. Height 11.5cm:4½in.

A charming poured wax dolls' house size doll with black bead eyes and painted black hair. The lower parts of all limbs are also poured wax. The original gauze frock, cape and bonnet trimmed with lace are worn. The general effect is very charming as the doll has been kept in its original box which carries an old note to the effect that it was given as a gift by Queen Victoria. The patina on one cheek is rubbed. Early nineteenth century poured waxes are not very commonly found so are bound to be of some interest.

£100

Poured Wax
Unmarked. c.1840. Height 46cm:18in.

The majority of poured wax dolls have inserted hair or, occasionally, a wig, so this example, with the hair laid on the wax scalp and then very lightly varnished or waxed is extremely interesting. The brows and lashes are implanted in the usual way. Note how the laid-on hair falls in very natural groupings on the neck.

The modelling of the head with its sharply turned position is good and the heavy treatment of the shoulders is much more vigorous than that usually seen on play dolls. The brilliant blue eyes are reminiscent of the work of the Montanari family. There is detailed modelling of the ears.

The gown and bonnet as well as the underwear are all exquisitely hand-stitched and embroidered. There are several spare garments including a nightgown and a pillow. Because of the doll's rarity a good price would be expected.

£350 — £375

Poured Wax
Unmarked. c.1860. Height 33cm:13in.

Only occasionally can the collector still find a doll in completely untouched original state. Even when a doll, such as this example, is in a somewhat sad condition the originality almost outweighs the fact that the buyer will need to spend some time on small repairs. The original blue silk brocade dress is extremely effective and its colour has been preserved as it was stored in its original matchwood box. The one leg is damaged but can be refixed. The head is in need of some cleaning. Almost all the implanted hair is missing and either a complete reinsertion of hair would be needed or the purist might prefer to cover the head with some kind of bonnet. The cost of reinsertion of hair would make the doll attractive to a dealer only at a fairly low price, though the general effect of the doll with its brilliant blue eyes, is most charming.

£200

Courtesy Christie's South Kensington

Poured Wax
Unmarked. c.1860. Height 48cm:19in.

A very typical English poured wax child doll with inserted fair hair and fixed blue glass eyes. The cloth body is hair-filled and has poured wax lower legs and arms. The doll is generally in good overall condition, but the head has been over-cleaned, giving a highly polished effect and spoiling the patina. The costume is attractive and consists of a chiné silk frock trimmed with coloured fringe and printed velvet. As the majority of wax dolls tend to wear dresses of white, the patterned dress would add to its attractiveness to a collector. The basic doll is unremarkable, but of obvious good quality, with its eyeleted limbs and inset lashes.

£200 – £250

Poured Wax
Unmarked. c.1865. Height 34cm:13½in.

The majority of poured wax dolls are given glass eyes, but in this example the eyes are painted. The heavy pink colouring of the wax would suggest that the maker was probably Pierotti. The lower arms and legs are also poured wax. The costume is effective but not superbly sewn, though the whole effect of the doll lying in a rocking crib that is also nicely decorated is pleasing as so completely original.

The hair is implanted in small groups and the complete doll is of a delicate construction. The condition of the complete object is excellent though the original squeaker, unusual in a poured wax, no longer works.

£225

Poured Wax
Indistinct mark on body. c.1868. Height 43cm:17in.

A poured wax made especially desirable by its very splendid original costume. It has brilliant blue eyes and an implanted mohair wig with a central parting, held by a plaited silk cord. The lower arms and legs are of poured wax and the stuffed body, unusually for this type of quality doll, contains a simple squeaker voice box. The blue silk evening dress is decorated with tatting and black velvet ribbons and rosettes. The net jacket is edged with blue velvet ribbon and lace. The matching cap is ornamented with fringing and pearls. The whole effect is completely charming and very colourful as a richly costumed miniature figure is presented that would hold an appeal for almost anyone interested in antiques as well as the basic doll collectors.

£325

Poured Wax
Unmarked. 1865-1875.Height 64cm:25in.

A poured wax lady doll made very impressive by the very complex original costume of rich cream coloured cut velvet with a very long cream silk train. The well-made shoes are marked 'M.G'. The head is nicely modelled in a creamy coloured wax that has developed a not unattractive patina. The hands are also modelled with slightly more than usual realism, as so often the makers of fine waxes seem to have lost interest over this aspect of the work. The blue eyes are fixed and the still abundant hair is inserted in groups. The lower legs are probably replacements, as the wax is a brilliant Pierotti type pink. Sometimes there are considerable differences in colour between parts of a doll that have always been covered with clothing and those left exposed, but in this case one would then expect the tops of the arms and the lower part of the shoulder plate to be a different colour also and this is not the case. It is possible to obtain replacement wax parts and a better colour match could therefore be obtained without too much difficulty, though the purist collector might not approve of such a solution.

£300 – £325

Poured Wax
Unmarked. c.1860. Height 64cm:25in.

A poured wax girl with a hand-sewn body suggesting, in combination with the style of the original costume, a date before 1875. The head is very postively turned to the side and is effectively modelled. The hair is implanted in small groups. Though the shoulder head is in good condition the limbs are very distressed and have been badly restored by an amateur. Both the limbs and the shoulder head are eyeleted. The original underwear is worn and the heavily embroidered dress adds considerably to the appearance. With good restoration this doll would again be an object of beauty. It is almost certainly of English origin.

£150 – £175

Courtesy Christie's South Kensington

Poured Wax
Unmarked. c.1870. Height 41cm:16in.

A poured wax child with implanted fair hair and fixed pale blue eyes. The hair-filled body has wax lower arms and legs. The mouth is more widely smiling than is usual in dolls of this type. A disfiguring crack runs across the face and whereas this type of damage does not as critically affect price as in a china doll, it does have considerable influence. The doll does not have any great charm as the modelling of the face is very shallow and a rather sweet and sugary effect is created. The original clothes are very well made.

£155 – £160

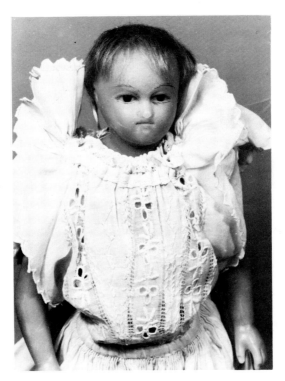

Poured Wax
Marked 'Meech'. c.1870. Height 33cm:13in.

Poured wax dolls are only occasionally marked and although their price depends in the main upon their quality and attractiveness an attributable doll is obviously preferred. This is marked 'Meech. Maker to the Royal Family. 6 Prize Medals Awarded. Old dolls cleaned and repaired. 50 Kensington Road, London'.

The head is interesting as it has very real character despite the flattened nose. The fine blonde hair is implanted, as are the lashes. The blue glass eyes are of an effective quality. The body is stuffed with hair and handsewn. The wax lower arms and legs were not given eyelets. The hands are particularly delicate and well-modelled for the small size.

The costume appears to be original but does not greatly flatter the doll. Meech worked in London between 1865 and 1891.

£200 – £225

Poured Wax
Unmarked. c.1880. Height 48cm:19in.

A well-modelled English poured wax doll of the Pierotti type with fair hair inserted in groups and fixed blue glass eyes. The head turning slightly to the left is often a characteristic of the work of this firm. Unfortunately the body has been renewed, presumably because of some damage, which will obviously depress the price. The costume is very attractive and consists of a long white lace-trimmed robe and a ribbon-trimmed and embroidered cream cloak and bonnet.

£225

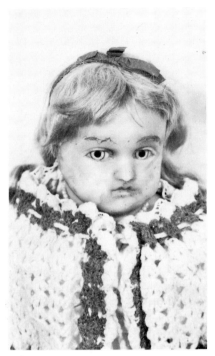

Poured Wax
Unmarked. c.1885. Height 56cm:22in.

Clumsy clothes such as those worn by this poured wax can completely ruin the effect of a perfectly acceptable doll. The fair hair is inserted in tufts and the head modelled as though turning to the left. The fixed eyes are pale blue. The brownish patina that has developed on the face has become rubbed and would have to be cleaned before the doll would again look completely presentable. If this patination is even it is much better to retain it, as it does give a doll a completely untampered-with appearance. The limbs are attached to the body through metal eyelets. A baby robe and a crochet jacket are worn.

£200

Courtesy Sotheby's

Poured Wax
Unmarked. Late 19th century. Height 49.5 and 43cm:19½ and 17in.

An interesting pair of poured wax dolls, thought to represent David Lloyd-George and his wife in wedding dress. The lady resembles the standard adult females made by the Pierotti family, though the man has much more individuality and is effective, if slightly sinister, with his very dark implanted hair. The lady is in good general condition but has a slight crack on the face. The man differs from the usual construction in that his hands are fixed to the cloth upper parts just above the wrists. He is made somewhat unattractive by the remains of a heavy dark brownish red colouring both on the face and the hands. The scale of this pair is so different that one cannot but wonder whether they ever left the manufacturer as a pair, as each doll is far better seen individually. It seems very possible that they were put together at a later date.

£500 – £550

Courtesy Phillips

Poured Wax
Unmarked. c.1910. Height 64cm:25in.

A poured wax lady wearing a faded green velvet dress with a decorative panel of bead- and sequin-embroidered yellow silk. The original underwear is worn and the very beautifully made cream silk shoes. The head, turning to the side, is realistically modelled with painted brows. The hair, of a very coarse texture, is applied in groups. The eyes are very pale blue. Though the arms look completely wrong because they are so absurdly out of scale, they are in fact original and of an identical colour wax, though they do detract considerably from the general appearance.

£150

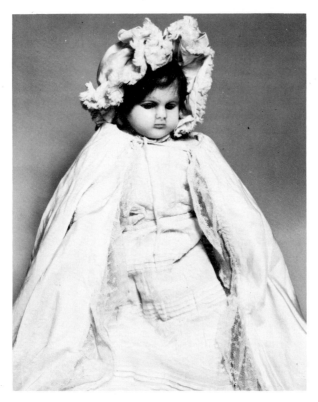

Poured Wax
Marked 'Lucy Peck'. c.1910. Height 51cm:20in.

Mrs. Lucy Peck worked in London around the turn of the century and up to c.1920. Her poured wax dolls are marked 'The Dolls Home or Dolls House, 131 Regent Street, London, W'. She sold and repaired wax dolls and, in addition, supplied German bisque-headed dolls, toys of all descriptions and books from her shop. This doll has blue glass eyes that are closed by the action of a wire that protrudes from the side of the torso. The auburn hair is implanted. The head of this doll is cracked and the limbs are also distressed, but the original costume with a cream silk hat is very lavish.

£200

Poured Wax
Unmarked. Modern. Height 58cm:23in.

It is usually by the poorer quality of the glass eyes that a reproduction poured wax can immediately be recognised. Most makers now incise their names in the wax or mark the torsos so there can be no possibility of a dealer selling such a doll as genuinely old. This example comes from one of the initial groups made by an English dollmaker and her work was not then marked, as the dolls were sold directly to collectors. In order to give a more convincingly antique appearance the metal eyelets were especially treated to given an old effect.

The mohair wig is implanted in the wax scalp in small groups. The fabric used for the torso and the upper arms and legs is of a peculiarly rough quality and quite unlike the more basic cotton or linen used by the old makers. The costume is not original to the maker and consists of a rather unpleasant almond green satin.

The high standard of craftsmanship seen in such reproductions obviously constitutes a trap for the unwary.

£40 new

AUTOMATA, MECHANICAL AND MUSICAL DOLLS

Figures that could imitate human movements in an amusing manner, while accompanied by music, fascinated antique collectors long before the appeal of ordinary dolls was recognised. Most of the finest and fully documented examples are already in established collections and, when sold, tend to move between a small group of specialists. Those appearing in the salerooms are of the more ordinary quality and would originally have been played in middle class homes to amuse the family. Some of those dealt with here have a double appeal, as the manufacturers utilised dolls' heads that were often of very good quality, so that a closed-mouth Jumeau or an F.G. lady's head is sometimes seen. If the movement or the musical box in the base of a mechanical figure is in any way damaged the price is very heavily affected as the cost of repair is sometimes so high as to be impractical.

Various mechanical and musical dolls were made at the end of the nineteenth century, including the American Webber singing doll and the well-known Edison Phonograph. The Phonograph doll is often found with a Jumeau head and would then attract the attention of both doll collector and gramophone enthusiast.

The Autoperipatetikos of 1862 is another walking doll that is often seen; its value depends very much on the quality of the head, as some of a very cheap-looking construction were used. Tin figures that move by means of a clockwork spring have a double appeal also, but this time to the collectors of tin. The musical marottes that play a tune when swung around are charming but not highly popular as they are difficult to display attractively, nice examples sometimes going through the salerooms for quite modest sums. Simple versions often incorporate a whistle or a voice box, together with numerous bells. The very simple types would be expected to fetch somewhere between £20 and £35 depending on the type of bisque head utilised and the condition of the costume.

A large variety of patents were registered in the second half of the nineteenth century regarding mechanical improvements. However, examples of these dolls only appear occasionally and have to be valued individually as the quality is very uneven; some makers utilised good heads while others made do with roughly pressed cardboard. In all mechanical and musical dolls, condition is all important as there is little value in an object of this type that does not work properly.

Automata
Unmarked. Early 19th century. Height 58cm:23in.

An effective early nineteenth century figure, possibly made as a window display piece. The complete costume is made of papier mâché with the exception of the lace and the ruffles at the neck. The hat is made of leather and given gold painted decoration. The head nods, the lower jaw, which is hinged, moves up and down and the eyes also move. An ornamental metal bell is carried in the right hand. The figure is contained in a glazed case. Such examples are outside the usual doll-collecting field and the figure is not sufficiently complex to be greatly desired by the collectors of automata. It would probably fetch a higher figure in a provincial general type of auction than in a specialist sale.

£200

Automata
Unmarked. c.1860. Height 34cm:13½in.

A fine example of a doll made by Theroude of Paris. It is wearing the original fashionable dress of pink and white satin trimmed with lace and cut gilt cardboard decoration. The head, in very good condition, is of waxed composition and the blue glass eyes are fixed. The original fair wig is braided. The clockwork mechanism contained under the skirt causes the doll to move around in a circle while the mandolin is 'played' and the head moves. The figure is protected by a glass shade.

£500 – £550

Automata
No visible mark. c.1865. Height 38cm:15in.

The firm of Steiner made dolls in Paris from the mid-nineteenth century and in 1862 patented an automatic talking *bébé*, followed by several other mechanical dolls, some of which were exhibited at the Paris Exposition of 1878. Walking dolls of this type have clockwork mechanisms and the voice box contained in the cone-shaped cardboard skirt concealed by the crinoline. They are wound from the side of the skirt and move along, raising the bisque forearms and crying 'mama'.

This example is dressed in the original pink silk and lace and has its original wig. The glass eyes are blue and the brows are painted in an almost orange shade, while the lips are slightly parted to reveal the teeth. Dolls of this type are almost invariably rather ugly but this is accepted as a characteristic and does not detract from the value of an example in such fine original condition.

£600 – £650

Courtesy Christie's South Kensington

Automata
No visible mark. c.1878. Height 36cm:14in.

A bisque-headed walking doll by Jules Steiner. This example is in poor condition as the lower arms are missing, as is one of the wheels on which the doll moves along when the key is wound. It does help considerably that the original woollen frock, trimmed with silk pleating, is still retained. The head is in good condition and has bright blue eyes and an open mouth with teeth.

£250 – £300

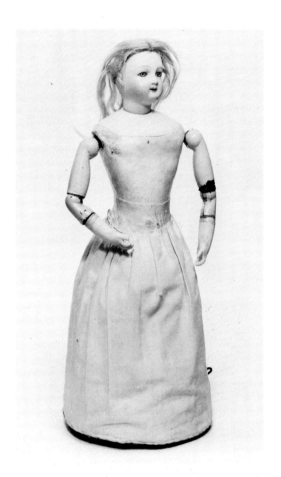

Automata
Marked on mechanism. c.1865. Height 38cm:15in.

Another example of the Steiner walking doll, though this time without the original costume. The eyes are blue and fixed and the mouth is slightly open to reveal the teeth. This is not one of the most attractive heads of this type though the good general condition of the figure is an advantage. The jointed metal arms can be clearly seen in this photograph with the bisque lower sections.

£400 – £450

Courtesy Christie's South Kensington

Automata
Unmarked head. c.1890. Height 39cm:15½in.

The firm of Steiner continually registered patents for improvements in mechanical dolls such as that in 1890 for walking dolls with a clockwork mechanism which he named 'Bébé Premier Pas' and 'Bébé Marcheur'. This example of Bébé Premier Pas in its original box with instructions in four languages is therefore of interest as the box is also marked 'J. St., mecanicien, breveté s.g.d.g.'

The bisque of the head is of good quality and the colouring is soft. The head is modelled with a solid pâte. The bright blue eyes are fixed in position. The carton body has rather odd waxed composition arms and legs not often used by this firm and probably replacements, the upper legs being of kid. The open mouth has six apparently replacement teeth as they are not of the usual type seen on mechanical Steiners. Despite its shortcomings the doll is still of great interest because of the box and the unusually good quality bisque.

£400

Automata and Mechanical
Marked 'Theroude et cie Paris'. c.1865. Height 38cm:15in.

This clockwork automaton was created by the company of Alexandre Nicholas Theroude who specialised in mechanical dolls, and worked in Paris. The doll stands on a metal platform that contains the mechanism which causes the head to turn from side to side as it moves on wheels. The doll has a papier mâché head with iris-less eyes, an open mouth with two teeth, painted hair, and a kid body. It is in the original costume of a silk and wool green checked coat, a straw hat and a net undercap.

£300 – £325

Courtesy Christie's South Kensington

Automata
Marked on heel. 1875. Height 24cm:9½in.

A mechanical walking Chinaman that is of interest as it is so fully marked, despite its lack of attractiveness as a figure. The features are painted and the moulded hair is supplied with a plait that emerges from a hole in the crown. The metal hands and feet are painted. The wooden body contains the mechanism that causes the legs to move forward on wooden rollers concealed under the feet. It is dressed in a black jacket and grey trousers. It is marked on the heel 'Patented Sept. 21 1875', a patent that was registered by Arthur Hotchkiss. Various characters were made such as Uncle Tom, Walking Jackass, General Benjamin Franklin Butler and the illustrated 'Heathen Chinee'. They were marketed by the firm of E.R. Ives, founded in 1866 at Plymouth, Connecticut, but eventually working at Bridgeport. In 1872 the name was changed to Ives & Blakeslee and this name is carried on the original box that contains the Chinaman. The green label is marked 'I B & Co'. It is very difficult to find American mechanical toys of this vintage in Europe and this is reflected in the price.

£300

Courtesy Christie's South Kensington

Automata
Marked on base. c.1865-1870. Height 28cm:11in.

An Autoperipatetikos with an attractive bisque woman's head with fair hair held in a snood and with the moulded collar decorated with a striped gilt and blue tie. The original dress in blue and silver is trimmed with braid and spangles. The base of the mechanism is marked 'Patented July 16, 1862 also in Europe 20th December 1862'. A considerable number of dolls of this type have survived so that despite their amusing qualities the price is kept fairly low.

£225

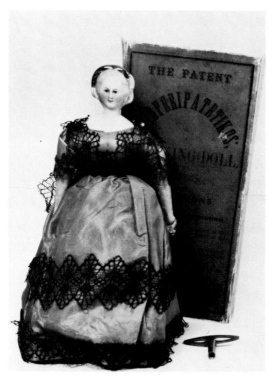

Automata and Mechanical
1862 label. Height 24cm:9½in.

A good and completely original example of a commercially costumed walking doll that moves on key-wound wheels concealed under the skirt. The lilac taffeta dress is trimmed with black lace. The lower arms are made of leather. The mechanism is still in perfect working order and the original tissue still holds the dress in position and wraps the doll in its box. The key is with the doll.

A variety of different heads were used on such Autoperipatetikoi and the quality and rarity of the head has an effect on the price, those with the most basic porcelain type head being the cheapest. Here the head is of good quality white bisque, referred to by collectors as 'parian': it has an effective lustre-decorated snood. Price is aided considerably by the original box

£250

Automata
Head unmarked. c.1865. Height 25cm:10in.

The number of dolls of this type that appear in the salerooms never ceases to surprise and says much for the strength of the mechanisms that have obviously withstood years of play. This version has an ornately moulded parian type head which gives added appeal. The blonde hair is held in place by a blue snood decorated with a pink lustre tassel and a green feather. The doll is contained in the original box with the working instructions, the original mauve silk dress is in fine condition, and the general effect of the figure is pleasing. The body is marked 'Patented July 15th 1862 also in Europe 20th December 1862' and also, interestingly, has the seller's label of 'Leuchars 3 Cheapside, London'.

Dolls of this type seen in salerooms over the last two years have been extremely unpredictable as to price as they seem to depend more than most on buyers' whims. This example reached £360 in the saleroom, whereas the previous example fetched only £230.

£250

Mechanical
Marked on base with 1862 label. Height 28cm:11in.

The original head of this Autoperipatetikos was obviously lost and a much later bisque head by Armand Marseille substituted, which completely destroyed the proportions. The new costume, very crudely made, also contributes to the unhappy effect. The leather arms are original and the basic mechanism, concealed under the skirt, is in working order.

As a more appropriate porcelain or parian shoulder head could be obtained without too much difficulty, a dealer would pay a reasonable price for such an object purely for the completely marked mechanism.

£100 – £120

Automata
Unmarked. Late 19th century. Height 48cm:19in.

An automaton of comparatively simple construction in the form of a standing Blackamoor plucking a mandolin as the head moves from side to side. The head is made of painted composition and the eyes are also painted. The legs are wooden and the musical movement is contained in the body. Figures of this type were made over a long period but can sometimes be attributed by makers' marks on the movement, which in this case is completely enclosed.

£200 – £250

Courtesy Christie's South Kensington

Automata
Head marked '5'. c.1900-1912. Height 43cm:17in.

A musical automaton of a bisque-headed woman standing at a piano. The head is bisque and of the quality of a good Parisienne with fixed eyes and a closed mouth. The carton body with painted metal hands is similar to those used by the Decamps family of Paris and an almost identical figure appears in a catalogue issued by the firm c.1912. The illustration, described as 'Fillette Piano', shows a very fashionably dressed girl wearing a feathered hat and a dress that is just calf length, in the actual style of the 1870s. The shoes and stockings appear identical to those worn by this doll. The catalogue drawing of the piano is somewhat simplified but completely recognisable, though the gilt coronet-shaped container on top of the piano originally held artificial flowers. Though in need of some slight attention, the mechanism of this figure is still in working order, while recostuming could be based on the illustration. A particularly fine attributable automata would then result with very little effort.

£850 – £950

Mechanical
Marked Simon and Halbig. c.1880. Length 41cm:16in.

This swimming doll with a clockwork movement in the stomach is often found either with the clothes disintegrating or without any at all. This pictured doll still retains the original blue cotton bathing-dress trimmed with lace, as well as a woven label of the exclusive French toy shop 'Au Nain Bleu, Bould. des Capucines 27 Paris'. The head is of good quality with fixed blue eyes. The limbs are of jointed wood but the hands are metal. The torso is a combination of cork and wood. When placed in the water the movements of the breast stroke are imitated.

£350 – £400

Automata
Unmarked. c.1885. Height 41cm:16in.

Musical toys of this type are only occasionally found with the entire figure of a doll on the top; much more frequent is a shoulder head or a flange-necked head. This attractive bisque has blue glass eyes, a blond wig, bisque legs and wooden hands. It wears an original eighteenth century style costume of a pink cotton coat and breeches. The musical box, which is in working order, is decorated with purple and green streamers, and as the stick is swung around the movement is activated. It seems possible that the wooden arms are replacements.

£180

Poupards and Novelties
Marked '4' on head. c.1880. Height 27cm:10½in.

A French bisque-headed poupard with fixed glass eyes and pierced ears. The decoration of the head is adequate and the two-tone mouth is closed. The cap is original and is decorated with braid. The costume, though original, is now very damaged and there would have been another layer to hide part of the handle. The musical movement still operates when the doll is swung, but the untidy general appearance would make for a low price.

£40 – £45

Courtesy Christie's South Kensington

Automata
Marked on head 'Deposé Tête Jumeau Bte. S.G.D.G.'.
Height 48cm:19in.

Here is a combination of a very desirable basic doll and an interesting automaton making for an appeal to two different types of collector. The doll has large fixed brown paperweight eyes with heavy painted brows, the colouring is pale and the mouth closed. The lower arms are of bisque. The costume is original and consists of a printed satin dress and hat edged with red lace and ribbon. A butterfly net is held in the right hand and a flower trimmed parasol in the left. A yellow butterfly, made of feathers, is suspended on a wire and this the doll attempts to catch in the butterfly net while her head moves from side to side. The musical movement is still in working order.

£550

Automata and Mechanical
Marked with an impressed clover and '5'. c.1890. Height 28cm:11in.

Any closed mouth German doll has appeal to collectors but this is especially attractive because when the body is squeezed the boy guitarist moves his arm and appears to 'play' his instrument. The eyes are large and fixed and the general appearance effective as so completely original. The impressed clover mark on the bisque head indicates that the doll was made by Limbach and it probably dates to the 1890s.

£160

Automata and Mechanical
Marked '103'. Late 19th century. Height 33cm:13in.

A bisque-headed doll, probably German manufacture, with fixed blue eyes, heavy brows and a closed mouth. The wood and wire body wears man's fancy dress in eighteenth century style and a tricorn hat. When the body is pressed a tune is played and the doll appears to draw a bow across the violin. An idea of the unpredictability of the prices obtained for such novelty figures that have no established scale of values is given by the fact that this figure in a May 1976 sale at Christie's fetched the startling figure of £280 while tne very similar doll previously illustrated from a Sotheby's sale that took place eight days later fetched only £125. The only noticeable difference seemed to be that one was dressed as a gentleman while the Sotheby's version was not!

£160

Automata
Unmarked. Early 20th century. Height 43cm:17in.

An automaton, probably of French origin, in the form of an elaborately dressed, seated clown with a smiling mouth revealing the moulded teeth. The clown plays a violin and as the musical box, concealed in the base, plays, the midget dances at the feet of the clown. Both figures have composition heads. The group is hauntingly sad because of the cleverly painted worn and strained face of the midget and though not a group one would personally like to live with, it is a change from the usual sickly sweet automata.

£650 – £700

Automata
Unmarked c.1905. Length 18cm:7in.

An amusing mechanical swimming doll that moves along on a key-wound clockwork base. The original costume is worn. The figure — probably German — is slightly spoiled by the very poor quality of the bisque head.

£50 – £70

Automata
Marked 'Made in West Germany'. c.1955. Height 27cm:10½in.

A pair of effectively constructed figures, one playing a drum and the other clashing cymbals. Both have composition heads with painted blue eyes and smiling mouths with modelled teeth. The bodies, feet and hands are made of metal and the figures are key-wound. The original cotton and velvet costumes are worn. The figures are of a better than usual standard for fairly recent mechanical dolls and carry the trademark of a monkey's head.

£15 – £20

CHINA SHOULDER HEADED DOLLS

The dolls with china heads and moulded hairstyles, and mounted on sawdust-filled fabric bodies, remained basically the same in construction from the 1840s to the 1920s. The early heads were made of glazed porcelain and the finest, often with a soft pink tint, were made at the Berlin porcelain factory. Large numbers of these were made by various German factories, many of whom did not bother to mark their work in any way. The basic doll, with short black hair and white, highly glazed face, is not of lasting interest to collectors once they own a good example, and this acts as a natural brake upon the price. Any addition to or variation on the basic, fairly short, black ringleted, hairstyle leads to higher prices, those with moulded flowers or very elaborate hairstyles being particularly considered. The simple dolls' house versions were made by the thousand and have consequently remained relatively cheap.

The so called 'parians', in reality usually white untinted bisque, were made in really surprising variety, especially as such a large number of moulds must have been necessary. Only rarely do examples of identical dolls occur and then usually in very different sizes. Many of these rival finely made porcelain figures in their perfection of detail, yet this type of doll, despite the rarity of individual pieces, does not generally fetch a high price. Their cold perfection and ornate formal hairstyles do not appeal greatly to the average collector.

Parians were followed by similar dolls made of delicately tinted bisque that attempted to imitate the colour of skin. The models were given a much softer appearance and resemble young girls, rather than the haughty ladies of parian. Very complicated decoration was frequently given to the head, including moulded earrings, necklaces, combs, flowers and lace collars. Again it is the amount of unusual decoration and rarity of certain moulds that affect the price, those with simple, short hairstyles and round, rather heavily coloured faces being the cheapest. Men dolls of this type in the larger sizes are very rare, as are those with swivel heads. A few coloured dolls were made, though their hairstyles are comparatively simple. Some damage to limbs has often to be accepted in this type as the legs swing together very roughly when moved, which leads to almost inevitable cracks and chips.

The moulded shoulder heads are one of the few types of doll that retain a good value if only the head is present. Many of these heads were originally sold separately for home assembly and consequently there are several collectors who buy just the heads alone. Any damage to the head is therefore of paramount importance.

Miniature versions, intended for dolls' houses, were made in a wide variety, ranging from elderly grey bearded gentlemen to young children. The detail on such dolls is often extremely fine and a complete family can fetch well above £200. Later dolls' house dolls of the type tend to be more highly coloured and were still advertised in toymen's catalogues in the 1920s, indicating how a doll that went generally out of fashion some forty years before could survive in a special area.

CIRCA 1835
ENGLISH

Courtesy Phillips

Porcelain
Unmarked. c.1840. Height 43cm:17in.

A very fine porcelain with slight modelling of the breasts on the very low cut shoulder plate. The whole shoulder head is tinted pink and the cheeks have a high colour, which is a characteristic of dolls of this type. There are three sew holes at the back and the front of the shoulder plate. The eyes are painted brown. The head is of the full domed type with four sew holes at the crown for the attaching of the hair wig. The body is made of fabric with blue leather lower arms, typical of the type found on slit heads. These highly coloured dolls with heavy cheeks were once thought to be of French origin, though this is by no means proven.

£400 – £450

Courtesy Sotheby's

Porcelain
Unmarked. c.1835-1840. Height 9cm:3½in.

A very fine German shoulder head mounted on a crudely made body. The features are modelled with unusual strength and the definition of the head is most striking. The dark brown hair is looped back over the ears. Had this doll been in a complete state, it would probably have been the finest porcelain in this guide but, unfortunately the complete shoulder plate is broken and all we are left with is a head to just below the neck. This example is however so fine that it would be a pity not to rebuild the shoulders. The price raised at auction among collectors for this fragment would be high, though it would be doubtful if any antique shop could obtain more than perhaps £50 for such a piece.

Heads of virtually identical type are found with the mark K.P.M. (Königliche Porzellän Manufaktur) inside the shoulder head and a complete doll of this type would obviously be very expensive.

£150 – £175

Courtesy Sotheby's

Porcelain
Unmarked. c.1840. Height 49cm:19½in.

Brown haired porcelains are only occasionally found, and this example is attractive because of the hair arranged in the early nineteenth century style with a coiled braid. The very white glazed head is mounted on a late nineteenth century body with composition limbs and the value therefore lies completely in the quality of the shoulder head. The doll is costumed in a modern black satin dress.

£200 – £250

Porcelain
Unmarked. c.1840. Height 29cm:11½in.

A doll with a porcelain head of the type made especially for attaching to a jointed wooden body. The specially shaped back of the shoulder allows for the wooden pegs that join the head to the body. The head has five moulded ringlets and the centre parted hair is looped behind the ears. The eyes are painted brown and the brows are grey. Both the lower arms and legs are made of porcelain and are attached by wooden pegs, articulation at the hip and thigh being given by ball and pin joints. One hand on this type of porcelain doll is usually moulded in a bent position, so that the figure can be given an object to carry. This was an unnecessarily expensive method of dollmaking, as it involved both the woodturner and the porcelain factory and was used for a comparatively short time, so that examples are not very easy to find.

£250 – £300

Courtesy Christie's South Kensington

Porcelain
Unmarked. c.1845. Height 14cm:5½in.

A potentially fine porcelain shoulder head, as the dark brown hair is swept into unusually thick coils over the ears and tied into an ornate plaited loop at the back. The eyes are painted in blue and have the red line above. The very thickly moulded head has six sew holes. The features have some character but are unfortunately marred by crazing in the glaze and by a very bad crack that runs down the chest and considerably depresses the price.

£70 – £80

Porcelain
Unmarked. c.1845. Height 34cm:13½in.

A very beautiful porcelain shoulder head that is delicately tinted and has slight modelling of the breasts. There are three sew holes at the back and front of the shoulder plate. The hair is drawn back from the face in two heavy loops and the ears are modelled. The hair is painted black and there are five well modelled ringlets. The eyes are painted brown. The body is of stuffed fabric with porcelain lower arms. The bonnet is a pleasing piece, but the general costume is in need of some attention.

£400 – £425

Porcelain
Unmarked except for '8'. c.1850. Height 48cm:19in.

A porcelain shoulder headed lady doll of particularly heavy pink colouring and very red cheeks. There are four sew holes at the crown of the head for the fixing of a wig. The eyes are bright blue with brown and red lines above the pupil. At the lower edge of the shoulder plate are three sew holes at the front and two at the back by which to attach the body. The china limbs are also provided with sew holes on this fine quality and unusual doll. The body is in a bad state of repair which makes the doll look much shorter than it should be. It was once thought possible that dolls of this very heavily tinted pink type were of French rather than German origin but there is at present no proof of this, merely the observation that they do differ considerably from the usual pink tinted German porcelains.

£400 – £450

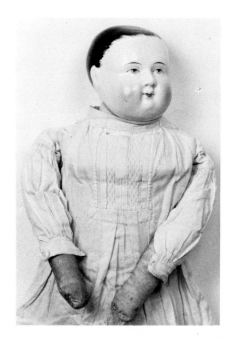

Porcelain
Unmarked. c.1850. Height 52cm:20½in.

Porcelain headed dolls modelled to represent boys with very short cropped hair are much scarcer than those in the form of ringleted ladies and the large size of this example is also an advantage. The eyes are painted in blue and the ears are more defined than is usual in porcelains. The dark brown hair ends with stylised brush strokes at the temples. There are some small imperfections to the glaze in this example and one with a much more perfect surface would obviously be even more desirable. The shoulder head is attached to the body by three sew holes front and back. The body, though old, is probably home-made, while the arms are also old replacements. A similar head mounted on a commercially made body with porcelain arms and legs would fetch an even higher price.

£180

Porcelain
Unmarked. 1840-1850. Height 54cm:21½in.

Porcelain shoulder headed dolls such as this with sawdust filled fabric bodies continued in production until the early twentieth century, though by this time it was mainly those in the smaller sizes that were still made. The value of a porcelain head therefore depends very much upon its basic quality, some being poorly moulded with little sharp definition, particularly of the hair.

This example has well-defined features and an expression that is more evocative of its period than is usually seen. The modelling of the hair is crisp and detailed, though the colour is the usual basic black. Unfortunately there is a bad firing fault on the lower left cheek, which detracts from the effect. Collectors and dealers once claimed that such faults as this, also specks of kiln dust, denoted an early doll but the manufacturers were perfectly capable, from the time that porcelain began to be used for dolls, of making a product that was completely free from such defects. Normally, a doll with a fault as bad as this would have been rejected before decoration but this one, for some reason, was passed and sold. Some doll buyers are not offended by such damage but the market would be very limited. The porcelain lower legs end in unusual grey and black boots and the doll has an attractive original white lace and muslin dress.

£100 – £125

Dolls' House Porcelain
Unmarked. c.1845. Height 10cm:4in.

Though this dolls' house porcelain shoulder headed doll is of the basic German type, it is most effectively dressed in fine cotton and muslin decorated with blue ribbon bows and tiny beads. The feet are modelled with flat heel-less boots and the hairstyle is winged. A great deal of the value here is dependant on the costume.

£50

Courtesy Sotheby's

Porcelain
Unmarked. c.1850. Height 43cm:17in.

An extremely beautiful porcelain shoulder headed doll with the added appeal of documentation, having been bought in Paris c.1850 for Mrs. Stoney of Raheeny, Co. Dublin, when a child, and called 'Miss White' in the family because of the whiteness of the face.

The head is very stylised with mannered painting of the eyes and is of a much slimmer type than usually encountered. On the crown is a painted black spot, the doll being of the type referred to by collectors as a Beidermeir. The applied plaited brown hair wig is very well made and delicate in construction. Sawdust-filled fabric body and pink leather arms. Such heads are usually attributed to a German source and this example was exported to France where it was purchased. The doll wears its original sprigged muslin dress and there are several other items of costume, but these are so poorly made that it is likely they were made by some child owner or a clumsy adult.

£300

Courtesy Christie's South Kensington

Porcelain
Unmarked. c.1850. Height 61cm:24in.

The rare porcelains of this type are often quite unattractive to the general collector of antique dolls and tend to be a very specialist interest. Considerable price variations are therefore seen and the absence of perhaps one dealer or collector who appreciates the type can mean a low price. This very large example is of added interest as it is accompanied by a framed letter stating 'The Dowager Lady Lyttleton enclosed to Mrs. . . .? a post office order for the amount of the price of the doll received for the Princess Royal . . . and is much approved. Windsor Castle, December 21st, 1850'. This proven connection with the Royal Family is bound to add in some degree to the value of an already unusual doll.

The German porcelain head is very heavily coloured and the cheeks even more so, which makes it especially interesting, if not particularly attractive. Pink tinted dolls are now popularly attributed to the Berlin factory as a few marked examples of softly tinted heads are known to have originated there, but without any mark the term Berlin can only be used in the widest sense as an indication of type. The eyes are painted blue and the bald head has three holes across the crown and one at the nape, all for the attachment of the well-made hair wig. The sawdust-filled body has tinted lower arms and legs with some damage to the top of one. The costume, which is original, is Welsh style with a black and red checked flannel open robe, petticoat, bonnet and hat and brown leather buckled shoes.

£800 – £1,000

Porcelain
Unmarked. c.1850. Height 6.5cm:2½in.

A porcelain headed doll mounted on a jointed wooden body and made very interesting because of its very small size. The head is pink tinted and the black hair is looped over the ears and drawn into a bun. The dress is contemporary and of blue silk. Although the head represents a woman, the dress is obviously that of a young girl. Miniature dolls almost form a collecting field in their own right and an unusually small example of a particular type will sometimes fetch more than one of medium size.

£60 – £65

Porcelain
Unmarked. 1850-1865. Height 38cm:15in.

As the limbs of porcelain dolls clatter together alarmingly when the figures are moved, a very large number of surviving dolls of this type have some damage to the hands and feet, and it is therefore a decided advantage when all the limbs are in perfect condition. This basic doll is of a very standard quality and the modelling of the hair is not particularly good. There are some slight kiln imperfections to the face, but the general effect is satisfactory. The boots are painted black and are of interest as they have very slight heels, indicating a date later than those with absolutely flat shoes.

The dress is recent and made of modern fabric. A reasonable example of a basic doll of this type.

£100

Porcelain
Unmarked. c.1855. Height 38cm:15in.

A china shoulder headed doll with the moulded black hair swept back from the face into a cluster of curls tied at the back of the head in the manner of the 1850s. The sawdust-filled body is very waisted and has lower arms of china; the feet are modelled with flat-heeled boots. The well-shaped ears are fully revealed. As so many dolls of this type have damaged hands or feet an example with an unusual hairstyle and in good condition is always desirable to collectors of this earlier type of doll.

£200

Porcelain
Unmarked. c.1860. Height 30.5cm:12in.

A head that appears of much better quality in a photograph than it is in fact. The modelling is acceptable for the type and, of course, boy dolls are more unusual in porcelain, but the pink colouring of the face is extremely unpleasant and of a rather 'jammy' texture that ruins the effect. The front of the hair is, in comparison, very well described. The shoulder has three sew holes front and back and the eyes are painted blue with a red line in the eyelids. The body is made of kid and the limbs are bisque with glazed lustre boots. These limbs together with a porcelain head are always an unhappy combination in the eyes of a collector.

£85

Courtesy Christie's South Kensington

Porcelain
Unmarked. c.1860. Height 66cm:26in.

An extremely impressive porcelain lady with much more character in the expression than is usual, the majority of porcelain dolls lacking individuality. The hair, being brown, rather than the usual black, is quite rare. It is held in a net snood and arranged with curls on the crown and the delicate brush strokes at the temples are a feature of better quality porcelains. This unusual head, in combination with the great size of the doll, makes it a very desirable acquisition. One of the legs is badly damaged but this is not as relevant on a doll of this rarity. The sawdust-filled cloth body is costumed in the original cream frock and cape.

£500 – £600

Porcelain
Unmarked. c.1860. Height 43cm:17in.

A porcelain headed Parisienne of the type usually described as Rohmer, with a gusseted kid body and porcelain lower arms. The hands are nicely tinted, but there are several fingers missing. The blue eyes are of the fixed type, with a blue line underneath, and there are the red spots to the nostrils, typical of the type. The shoulder is unfortunately very badly damaged and has been roughly glued together, which considerably affects the price. The original costume is of pale cream muslin and silk, decorated with pink silk ribbon and black velvet ribbon. The original side-buttoned light brown boots are worn.

£200 – £225

Porcelain
Unmarked. c.1860. Height 46cm:18in.

Parisiennes with glazed porcelain heads of this type are often attributed to Rohmer, a company run by Mlle. Marie Rohmer in Paris from 1857-1880, though it is possible that similar dolls were made by other firms. The porcelain headed Parisiennes are hardly beautiful, as their faces are so flat and little effort was put into realistic modelling, but they do have great charm, and most collectors would require at least one example. The heavily painted nostrils are particularly characteristic. The original wig is of dark brown human hair and the body is of gusseted white leather. The dress is contemporary and of dark blue ribbed silk.

The majority of surviving examples tend to be fairly small, so this, despite its lack of real beauty, would be expected to command a good price, but unfortunately this doll has a hair line crack running under the chin which obviously depresses the price.

£260 – £285

Porcelain
Unmarked. c.1860. Height of shoulder 7.5cm:3in.

It would appear that these two-faced heads were especially made for use on heavily weighted pincushion bases, as each example encountered in its original state has been in this form. This is a particularly fine example of the type, as the modelling is very crisp and the colouring effective. Usually, in a two-faced doll, the two sides share a similar bonnet, and in this case the youthful face is moulded only with hair, which called for a little more skill. The older face is extremely effective. The heavy base is filled with emery powder that kept pins free from rust. Similar versions are seen but with rather less detail.

£400

Porcelain
Unmarked. c.1860. Height 37cm:14½in.

An interesting porcelain shoulder head modelled as a boy, with effective brush strokes to the sides of the face and forehead. The eyes are blue and of the painted type, and the features are crisply modelled. The head is mounted on a later commercially made machine-sewn body. It is sometimes surprising how little a wrong body effects the price in a saleroom, though a dealer would find that it told heavily against the doll.

£150 – £165

Porcelain
Marked '10'. c.1865. Height 41cm:16in.

Hair waved at the front in this style became fashionable from the late 1850s but the coils, braids, switches, waterfalls and frizettes are particularly associated with the mid-60s. Once particular moulds were made, dolls continued to be produced from them for some time and dating by hairstyle can only be approximate. This example has well modelled ears that are pierced for earrings. Only a relatively small number of porcelains have pierced ears, as the glaze tended to run into them during firing and their later drilling out can be seen on many dolls. The eyes are blue painted but without the red line usually associated with better quality porcelains. The actual porcelain used for this example is of a very heavy type and there are a number of firing imperfections, such as kiln dust and some faults in the glaze. The bust is modelled with more realism than usual. The earrings appear original. The body is old but probably not original and the arms appear to be old replacements. Basically the buyer is therefore obtaining a head.

£200

Porcelain
Unmarked. c.1870. Height 32cm:12½in.

A porcelain shoulder headed lady doll of the later type with short hair and blue painted eyes without a red line. The body is of blue fabric with pipeclay type lower parts to the limbs. Such pipeclay limbs are found in particular on the bodies that were made for English dolls during the First World War though this head is of the German type. The price of the doll is low, as collectors would prefer dolls of this type with porcelain limbs.

£25 — £30

Bisque
Unmarked. c.1880. Height 42cm:16½in.

A well tinted bisque shoulder head with inset glass eyes and a swivel neck. The fair hair is well moulded and there is a hole pierced through the curls on the crown to allow for the fixing of a small ornament. The face is of the fuller type and has a gentle expression. The ears are pierced. Only occasionally do shoulder heads with so many interesting features appear in the salerooms and this example would appeal to many collectors.

£300 – £400

Courtesy Sotheby's

White Bisque
Unmarked. c.1875. Height 20cm:7¾in.

A shoulder headed bisque lady doll of the type known as parian to collectors. The hair is well modelled and held in place with a blue moulded band. The ears are pierced and green glass earrings are worn. The bisque and the decoration are of most acceptable quality and the effect is heightened by the original brown flounced crinoline type dress. The body is sawdust-filled and the lower limbs are the usual white bisque.

£100 – £125

Bisque
Unmarked. c.1855-1860. Height 13cm:5in.

A pair of dolls' house shoulder bisques in completely original condition. The doll in the foreground wears a two coloured soft woollen dress and has black lower legs to represent black stockings. The other, in a black skirt, wears black painted boots. Fairly early dolls' house dolls are always in demand since even the smallest dolls' house needs a surprisingly large number of dolls if the atmosphere of a Victorian household is to be achieved.

£25 – £35 the pair

White Bisque
Unmarked. c.1855. Height 22cm:8½in.

A white bisque lady doll of the type popularly referred to as parian, made up as a pincushion figure. The bisque is of the more coarse quality but the hair, in its waterfall-type style, is effectively modelled. The arms are of the same material. The original cream and black velvet and silk ribbon dress is worn with gilt decoration to the belt and bangles. Dolls with damaged legs were sometimes assembled in this way, but others were of this original intention.

£100

White Bisque
Unmarked. c.1855. Height 23cm:9in.

A white bisque shoulder headed lady doll with blonde hair enclosed in a net which is held in place by a black band and further decorated with a blue bow over each ear. All this detail is, of course, moulded in the bisque. The very low bust and deeply sloping shoulders indicate the comparatively early date of the original mould. The body is made of cotton and filled with sawdust; the limbs, which should also have been of white bisque, are broken, thus considerably lowering the price of the doll. Though the head is well modelled, the quality of the bisque in this example is very poor, as it is granular and unpleasant to the touch. The costume is partly original but poorly made, with the exception of the cape.

£80 – £90

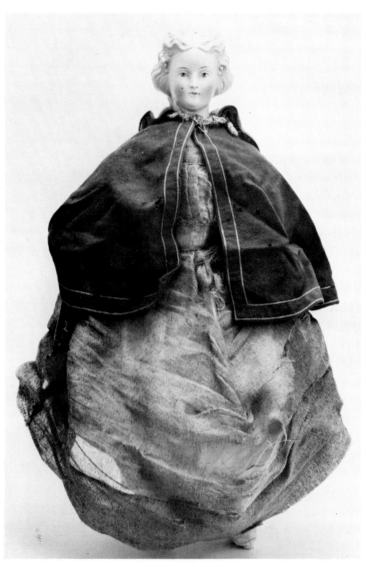

Courtesy Sotheby's

180

Bisque
Unmarked. c.1865. Height 61cm:24in.

Delicately tinted bisque headed dolls of this type are most frequently found in smaller sizes, so that the height of this example creates an immediate impression. Because of the elegance of the modelling of such heads early collectors believed that they were of French origin, but it is now generally accepted that they are of German manufacture. This hairstyle is particularly elaborate even for dolls of this decidedly decorative type, and is moulded with ornate braids, loops and waves, ending in a chignon at the neck. The coiffure is further dressed with ropes of moulded gold lustred beads. The eyes are painted blue.

The cloth body, in somewhat poor repair, has red leather arms, one of which is present but detached. The original scarlet woollen cloak is worn, together with a gauze dress in a very tattered state. The underwear is original and there is a particularly well-made hooped petticoat, constructed as a correct miniature garment. Though dolls of this type were not very popular in the late 60s and very early 70s, they are now again becoming popular, though prices at individual sales are still rather unpredictable in comparison with the later jointed bisques.

£350 – £375

182

Bisque
Impressed '1064 x 3/o'. c.1875. Height 8cm:3¼in.

A shoulder head of the tinted bisque type sometimes described as 'blonde bisque'. The eyes are painted blue and the moulded hair is blonde. The head is in good condition but the modelling of the hair is not well defined and the face is a little over sweet. It is difficult to find replacement bodies for such heads and this is not of sufficiently fine quality to hold its own purely as a shoulder head and a high price could not be expected.

£20 – £25

White Bisque Bonnet Head
Marked '6'. c.1880. Height 31cm:12¼in.

During the 1870s the German makers of bisque shoulder heads began working towards a doll of a much more child-like appearance. Though the modelling of the face at first changed but little, an air of childhood was given by the addition of moulded bonnets. Heads of this type vary considerably in decoration, some being gilded and having moulded feathers. The colouring and the quality of the bisque also varies, this example having the cheek tinting very roughly applied. I know of no bisque bonnet dolls of really fine quality, such as that seen in the early parian type heads, and they were fairly obviously the last flicker of an outdated medium.

This doll has the well-modelled inside brim of the bonnet painted in blue and gold with a blue bow under the chin. The stuffed body has porcelain lower arms and legs ending in painted green boots and red garters. Porcelain limbs with a bisque head are always unsatisfactory, it being doubtful whether the head and body actually belong together. Heads of this period were quite frequently sold loose and were an obvious replacement for the head of a child's porcelain doll. Such marriages seem to bother the general saleroom buyers far less than they did a few years ago.

£120

White Bisque
Unmarked. c.1860. Height 9cm:3½in.

Dolls' house inhabitants made with moulded bonnets and hats are not very often found and this doll is especially good, as it is a fairly early example of the type. The shoulder headed doll with stuffed fabric body wears a moulded yellow boater with a pink lustre feather. The moulded hair is dark brown. The original costume is worn.

£80 – £85

White Bisque
Unmarked. c.1890. Height 25cm:10in.

A pair of basically fairly ordinary white bisque shoulder headed dolls of a rather coarse bisque, made attractive by their ostentatious costume and amusing period effect. One lady carries a dainty handkerchief and the other a muff. Both have painted blue eyes and wear wigs of mohair. The bodies are fabric with sawdust filling and have white bisque lower arms and legs. They are both of German origin, and large quantities of similar dolls are found in dolls' house size.

£70 – £75

Bisque
Marked 'E 2 D'. c.1860. Height 33cm:13in.

An extremely unusual bisque shoulder headed doll that is most probably of French manufacture though this is not certain. The eyes are painted bright blue, but carelessly, so that one was not even painted in the socket provided. The fair hair is moulded but without any detail and the general effect of the doll, whose body is of the straight limbed leather type, is not very pleasing. It has a certain rarity value, but is a doll that a dealer would find somewhat difficult to place.

£180

Tinted Bisque
Unmarked. c.1865-1875. Height 46cm:18in.

This pink tinted bisque shoulder head is made more interesting because of set-in glass eyes, unusual in this type of doll. The short blonde curls are moulded and the head is turned to the right. The fabric body is well-shaped and sawdust-filled. All the lower parts of the limbs are made of bisque and the legs are finished by very attractive blue boots. These high heeled boots, with maroon tassels and black toes and heels, indicate a late nineteenth century date. The doll is undressed. The value is approximately halved by the bad crack that runs up the front of the shoulder plate and almost completely around the neck. A doll with this degree of damage would be very difficult to sell from a shop, unless it was first restored. The price suggested is for the example as it stands and disregards a potential value after costuming and restoration.

£125

Bisque
No visible mark. c.1870. Height 44.5cm:17½in.

A tinted bisque shoulder headed child-style doll of better than average quality for the type. The eyes are painted blue and the light brown hair is more unusual than the fair type. The stuffed body has lower arms and legs of bisque while the moulded boots are an attractive pink lustre. The value of this doll is considerably increased by the effective printed cotton frock that is an acceptable miniature garment of the early 1870s. The matching sun bonnet is equally well made. All the limbs are in good condition, which is unusual for the type and adds to the value.

£200

Bisque
Unmarked. c.1870. Height 33cm:13in.

A tinted bisque shoulder headed doll in unusually good general condition and without the chips and damage to feet etc., often associated with dolls of this type. The head is of the more basic type with centre-parted, moulded fair hair with well defined curls surrounding the head. The stuffed fabric body has bisque limbs with flat-heeled painted boots and pink garters. The effect of a not particularly exciting doll is improved by the original white muslin flounced frock trimmed with mauve ribbon.

£150 – £200

Bisque
Unmarked. c.1865-1870. Height 28cm:11in.

Few glass eyed shoulder head bisques were made, as the insertion of glass eyes through the fairly narrow neck was not easy. This glass eyed example, with a hairstyle of the mid-50s, has boots with small heels indicating a manufacture possibly as late as the 1870s. The body, of fabric with sawdust filling, is original and the doll is an indication of how heads in somewhat outdated styles continued to be used for some time. The boots are pink lustre and the socks are glazed in white with purple garters painted in a scalloped pattern. Frequently there is some damage to the limbs of dolls of this type, so it is refreshing to find an example where the whole figure is in perfect condition. The colouring of the head is pleasing and the brows are delicately painted.

£250

Author

Bisque
Unmarked. c.1870. Height 46cm:18in.

This doll is rare because of the swivel fitted to the neck, enabling the head to be turned. This is a method commonly used on Parisiennes, but only occasionally in dolls with a moulded hair style. The value is also enhanced by inserted glass eyes, the positioning of these through the narrow neck aperture being a slow process. The head itself is of delicately tinted pink bisque and has pierced ears. The crisply moulded hair is parted in the centre and drawn into a bun at the back. The fabric body is sawdust-filled and the lower parts of the limbs are bisque. The moulded boots are painted in grey and black and have small heels which suggest a date in the 1870s. The general finish of this doll is very high, as instanced by the delicate tinting of the white bisque of the arms, a refinement that is usually omitted in the cheaper types.

The original costume consists of a blue muslin frock with a white muslin overdress and pinafore, but although this is charming, it hardly matches the quality of the doll.

£370 – £400

Bisque
Unmarked. c.1875. Height 28cm:11in.

A very effectively costumed Scottish boy in original state. The head, of the so-called blonde bisque type, has fair moulded hair and blue painted eyes with a red line just above the eye itself. The body is of the waisted fabric type that is sawdust-filled. One of the feet is damaged, but this would not affect the price too considerably. Though of German manufacture, large numbers of these figures are found in Scottish costume, probably dressed in Britain.

£85

Bisque
Unmarked. c.1875. Height 28cm:11in.

A blonde bisque shoulder headed girl doll with moulded hair arranged
in two plaits on the crown and decorated with two black painted bows.
The head is of very acceptable quality under the grime. The figure is
made much more desirable by the inset glass eyes, unusual in dolls of
this type, as they were not easy to plaster in place. The lustre-decorated
boots are also an indication of a better quality doll of the type. The
original wool dress is worn and is trimmed with purple velvet ribbon.
Although its state of repair is not good, the costume is quite retrievable
with some disguise and general tidying.

£200

Bisque
Unmarked. c.1900. Height 16.5cm:6½in.

A dolls' house man with a moulded fair moustache and hair with painted blue eyes. The body is sawdust-filled fabric and the lower arms and legs are bisque. One foot is damaged and the original, but not very well fitting, suit is worn.

£30 – £35

Bisque
Marked 'K' in bell and '3'. c.1900. Height 30.5cm:12in.

The firm of Kling, whose factory was in Thuringia, marked their bisque and porcelain shoulder heads with an impressed bell. This doll is interesting as it has glass eyes and any marked examples with glass eyes, rare in any type of shoulder head with moulded hair, are highly collectable. The high tinting of the bisque is typical of the marked Klings but the modelling is much more realistic than usual. The expression is beautiful and the richly coloured blonde hair is crisply modelled. The body is of the small waisted sawdust-filled type with bisque lower arms and legs. One leg is missing and there is some damage to the other. The original hand-stitched underwear is worn with a black wool skirt trimmed with velvet ribbon, a white blouse and a red bolero.

£200

Bisque
Marked '1062H 4'. c.1885. Height 44.5cm:17½in.

A bisque shoulder headed doll dating to the late nineteenth century when a more child-like image was aimed at by the manufacturers. The eyes are painted blue and the blonde hair has very well defined curls, the fringe modelled with some realism. The stuffed body is typical of the type, with bisque lower arms and legs. The original dress is of white muslin with pink silk bows. Such dolls are only occasionally marked, so a marked example such as this has an obvious advantage.

£150 – £200

Courtesy Christie's South Kensington

Bisque
Unmarked. c.1885. Height 33cm:13in.

The theme of a large doll carrying a smaller one always has some appeal and this example is effective, as the whole arrangement is in the untampered-with condition that collectors like. The mother is of the basic tinted bisque shoulder headed type, with moulded hair held in place by a black band, and the unusual addition of pierced ears. The eyes are painted blue. The stuffed body has bisque arms and legs though one leg is missing. It is costumed in red and black flannel as a Welsh woman. The baby doll, here shown carried on the back, also has moulded fair hair.

£140

Courtesy Sotheby's

Bisque
Unmarked. c.1855-1890. Height 30cm:11¾in.

A shoulder bisque made in Germany and of a basic type that could be dressed either as a boy or a lady. The eyes are larger than is often found on this type and are very strongly suggested, but the modelling of the hair lacks crispness. The body is fabric and the limbs bisque. A grey reconstructed alpaca suit is worn.

£80

Bisque
Marked on shoulder '153-10'. c.1890. Height 61 cm:24in.

The photograph does not flatter this doll, as it has an extremely effective, if not unusual head, with the moulded fair curls associated with blonde bisque dolls. Similar figures of this type were made by Simon and Halbig. The eyes are painted blue and the lower arms are made of bisque. The effect of the head is somewhat spoiled by the poor quality leathercloth body which is in a bad state of repair. The provincial costume is original.

£160 – £185

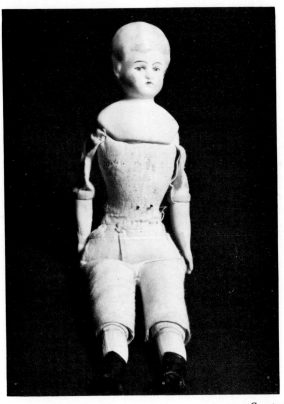

Bisque
Marked '120/90'. c.1900. Height 25cm:10in.

A bisque shoulder head illustrating very clearly how the general quality of dolls deteriorated once they were outside the interest of the most fashionable children. Here the hair has virtually no modelling or definition and relies for its effect purely upon colour. The eyes are painted in blue and the lower limbs are bisque. The body is made of cheap pink muslin.

£60

Courtesy Sotheby's

Bisque
Unmarked. c.1890-1910. Height approx. 14cm:5½in.

Part of a family of nine dolls' house inhabitants. They are partly redressed in eighteenth century style and unfortunately cotton wool etc. has been glued to the heads of some of the most interesting men dolls, so that the group would need some general cleaning and restoration before sale. Under the additions are some extremely good dolls' house figures, such as an old grey bearded gentleman and a few lady dolls with well-shaped hair. A few of the figures have missing limbs, but as it is difficult to find complete dolls' house families of approximately the same scale, they almost invariably fetch a good price.

£250

Courtesy Phillips

Bisque
Impressed 'Germany'. c.1930. Height 4cm:1½in.

Large numbers of shoulder heads such as these are now discovered by the 'diggers' who excavate Victorian rubbish tips. Unfortunately the time spent in the earth has usually marked such heads badly and the brown iron stains in particular are impossible to remove. The painting of the features has also usually been spoiled. Though such a head has some small value it would be of virtually no interest to the doll collector unless in pristine condition.

£1 – £2

RAG DOLLS

The term rag, in doll collecting, usually includes not only dolls made of this actual substance but also those made of pressed felt or velvet which was often mounted on a buckram or card mould. This type of doll has not interested many collectors until quite recently, when there was an upsurge of interest and some of the better types now command respectable prices. They are never likely to become as generally popular as china dolls, because the nature of the materials means that the faces quickly become discoloured and are not always easy to clean.

Home-made rag dolls, constructed from scraps of old fabric, have a history which dates to the beginnings of civilisation. It is a method of dollmaking which has continued throughout the centuries and any dolls in good condition and dating to the eighteenth century or before are desirable, though even here prices vary widely, as this type would only appeal to a small core of collectors.

Interesting rag dolls were made in America by Izannah Walker and later, in stockinet, by Martha Chase. The Americans were the first to introduce designs colour-printed on fabric, to be made up at home, and the Arnold Print Works is particularly associated with this type of doll, though there were many imitators, both in America, and in England, where Dean's Rag Book Company was the most famous producer. Pressed face dolls were made by Norah Wellings to a very high standard up until the 1950s, and those made by Chad Valley were also of good quality and included some portraits of the Royal Family. In Italy, Lenci made pressed felt dolls which are memorable because of the effective costumes, while in Germany, dolls made by Steiff were characterised by a seam that ran down the middle of the face.

The prices of rag dolls fluctuate considerably, even between sales held in the same week, according to the whims of collectors. Dealers will only pay low prices for rag dolls as they are not easy to sell, the continental and Japanese buyers having little interest in them as yet. Those made by Lenci seem to be the most stable in price, though even here surprising variations between sale prices occur.

The Boudoir dolls, with their long gangling legs and alluring faces, were made in the 1920s and 30s purely for the amusement of adults and those costumed in the fashionable clothes of their period are often bought now by non-collectors as amusing decorative pieces. Those dolls dressed in retrospective eighteenth century costume are not very popular, though their look of antiquity often leads the general antique dealer to offer them for sale at highly inflated prices.

Fabric
Unmarked. c.1850. Height 24cm:9½in.

A pair of very beautifully made fabric dolls, probably of commercial construction, with exquisitely stitched separated fingers and toes. These dolls are not in the least like the usual rather plump fabrics, but are slim and extremely delicate, with embroidered features. The hair is made of wool and the complete dolls are constructed from black twill. The costumes are made of cotton, silk and wool. These very effective figures are quite outside the order of the usual rather clumsy rag dolls but rarely fetch the prices they would seem to deserve, as they are unattributable.

£100

Fabric
Unmarked. 19th century. Height 28.5cm:11¼in.

An engaging fabric Portuguese man with a crudely embroidered head, but made attractive by the colour and cut of the brocade doublet and leather boots. Despite its obvious age, historical interest and the fine fabrics used in the costuming, figures such as this which cannot be fitted neatly into some collecting slot have a very limited value in monetary terms.

£15 – £20

Courtesy Sotheby's

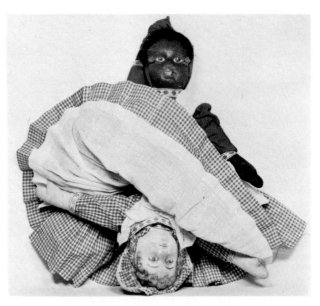

Fabric
No visible mark. c.1902. Height 32cm:12½in.

A topsy-turvy doll of the type patented by Albert Bruckner in 1901 and described as a face "composed of two or more layers of suitable material the outer layer being preferably of suitable textile fabric, while the inner layer or layers are made of paper or other suitable material. The outer layer in flat condition is first printed in suitable colours in imitation of the colours of a natural face ... and the two are then moulded together ... below the face is an extension forming the neck ... the completed face is glued or otherwise securely attached to the stuffed dummy-head". The patent was registered in the U.S.A., Albert Bruckner living in New Jersey. The mark is usually found on the end of the neck section and is probably concealed by the clothing in this example.

The lithographed colouring is very soft and attractive and the costume in good condition. Such dolls are very much collected in the States and the price that was obtained for this example suggests a buyer for this market as fabric dolls are still very undervalued here.

£130 – £150

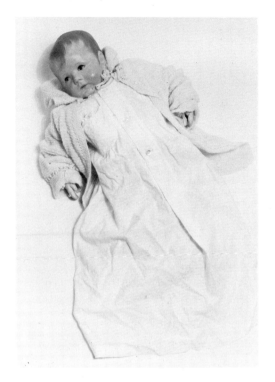

Fabric
Marked on feet 'Made in Germany Kathe Kruse 496'.
c.1910. Height 48cm:19in.

Kathe Kruse began to make dolls in Germany in 1907 and to market them around 1910. The heads were made of muslin, the reverse side of which was specially treated. The heads were painted under the direct supervision of the designer herself and are rendered with some realism. This realism is further accentuated in this example by the sand which was used to weight the body and make it feel like a real baby when handled. The doll wears its original gown though the knitted coat was probably added later. The general condition is good and the whole doll is a fine example of the wide awake type with its painted eyes glancing to the side. It is contained in the original box, which is still in acceptable condition.

£250 – £300

Courtesy Phillips

Fabric
Unmarked. c.1905. Height 43cm:17in.

A printed commercially-made rag doll wearing lace-printed combinations and red stockings. Blue and pink ribbons are 'threaded' around the garments. The head is well printed and were the doll marked in any way the price would be higher but it is at present not possible even to give a tentative attribution. The doll is accompanied by a set of particularly well made clothes.

£25 – £30

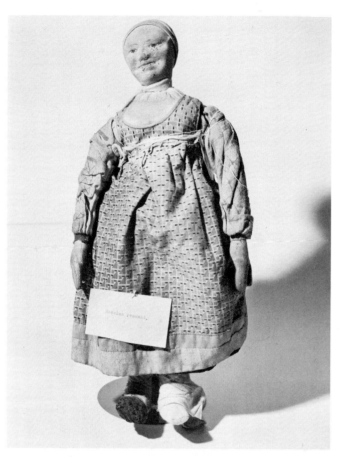

Fabric
Unmarked. c.1910. Height 37cm:14½in.

A Russian peasant woman with a fabric face moulded over a mask of composition, and with painted features and blue eyes. The body is rag and the lower legs are fabric-bound. The doll wears a faded blue and red cotton pinafore, a pink scarf on the head and one plaited straw slipper. Such folk-type costume dolls do not appeal greatly to the vast majority of collectors and the price is therefore kept quite low.

£20 – £25

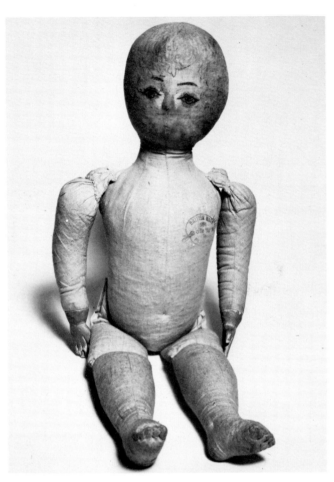

Courtesy Phillips

Fabric
Marked on body. c.1915. Height 58cm:23in.

Before this example appeared in the saleroom, the author was only familiar with the work of Adelaide McMillan from the patent office specification for her design for a rag doll, which was registered in 1915, and this doll, though of no great monetary value, is of great interest to collectors of English dolls made during the First World War. The torso is marked with a palette printed 'British Made. The Mac Doll British Made. Patent No. ?' On the back the patent number is legible and reads 'Pat. No. 10538 McMillans'. The body is machine-sewn and the hands are of carved wood. The features are painted in a very free artistic manner. The doll was made, according to the specification, at Workington, and cork was used as the stuffing material. 'The head and trunk are made of four pieces of cloth which are sewn together along their edges. To facilitate the formation of the neck two portions are removed from the front section and the edges are joined . . . the arms are joined to the body by a tab and a web formed in the trunk, the web limiting the upward movement of the arms. The upper end of each leg is sewn to form a tab which is sewn into the bottom trunk'. As an illustration of this particular doll has not previously been published, it seems worthwhile giving the specification in some detail.

£30 – £40

Fabric
Marked with seal. c.1925-1930. Height 48cm:19in.

Though of recent manufacture, this doll is unusual in that it carries some mark whereas the majority of the glamorous boudoir type dolls are completely without any identification. A gold seal is tied to the hand inscribed 'La Poupé d'Amour. Marque Deposée. The costume is of black silk with gold braid decoration. The lower legs and arms are made of composition and the moulded high heeled shoes are painted in gold. The face is of the moulded mask type with silk covering and the very long lashes are applied. The whole figure is in good condition.

£20 – £25

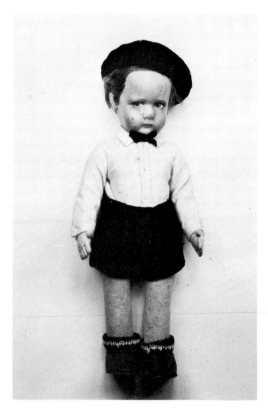

Courtesy Christie's South Kensington

Fabric
Marked Lenci. c.1923. Height 41cm:16in.

The early twentieth century is characterised by the number of dollmakers who claimed to make 'art' dolls of various kinds. In the case of the Lencis, this referred to the characterisation that was put into the pressed felt faces, which were all made with the painted eyes, with highlights, glancing to the side. The dolls were called 'Lenci', as this was the nickname of the wife of Enrico Scavini, who manufactured the figures. Great care was given to the effective costuming of the dolls, and this example wears the original black and white outfit. The eyes are painted in brown and the wool hair is sewn to the head in tufts.

£65

Fabric
Marked Lenci. 1921. Height 61cm:24in.

A painted felt doll with its label 'Lenci Di. E Scavini packed September 8th 1921'. This doll is very much in the idiom of the 20s and is not as immediately appealing to the doll collector as the child dolls with their sulky expressions. The body is of felt, the hands have the characteristic joining of the middle fingers, the brown painted eyes look to the right. The blonde wig is made with ringlets at the side and a plaited bun at the back. The whole figure is in fine original condition and a young woman's outfit of felt appliquéd frock with apron, felt hat with flower and lace trimming and mauve wooden high heeled shoes, is worn.

£60

Fabric
Marked Lenci. c.1925. Height 42cm:16½in.

This boy doll of pressed felt has a fair wig, painted features and brown eyes, which glance to the right. The middle fingers of each hand are joined, a characteristic of a Lenci. The original costume of brown shorts with a matching cardigan and leg warmers is worn. The Lenci trademark was registered by Enrico Scavini in Britain in 1922. These dolls were made in Italy by Italian craftsmen and each was given individual attention.

£55

Fabric
Marked with metal button. c.1913. Height 30.5cm:12in.

The Steiff Knopf im Ohr (button in ear) was registered as a trademark for cloth-jointed dolls in 1905. This company, begun by Margarete Steiff, worked in Wurttemberg and made a wide variety of soft toys and animals. The Highlander was advertised in Gamages catalogue for Christmas 1913 in 17, 20 and 24 inch sizes, the largest costing 7s.6d. They were described as 'Character dolls. Individual features, Unbreakable, Jointed, Comical, Soft Stuffed'. This example, with the characteristic seam running down the centre of the face, is in very nice condition, with the felt face completely unmarked. Many fabric dolls are spoiled because of the natural discolouration of the fabric, so that a well-kept example, especially with the original button, is a good addition to any collection.

£25

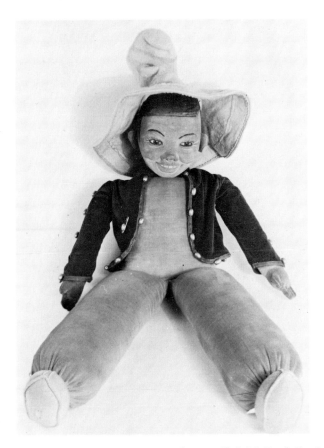

Fabric
Unmarked. c.1935. Height 71cm:28in.

A Mexican boy doll whose face is made of moulded velvet over a base shape. The fixed eyes are of brown glass and the open mouth is smiling to reveal the teeth. This is a doll that is completely typical of the work of Nora Wellings and probably once carried a sewn-on label. The original costume of velvet is still in good condition. Despite the skill used in their construction and their amusing effect, these English dolls are still very much a minority interest.

£30 – £45

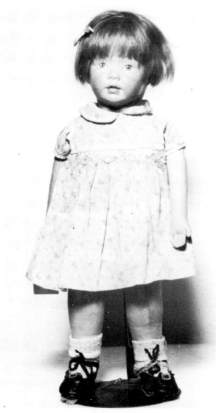

Courtesy Beatrice L. Wright, Phoenixville, Pa.

Fabric
Marked on head. c.1920. Height 46cm:18in.

A fabric doll which was designed by Louise R. Kampes at Atlantic City, New Jersey. These dolls had moulded mask faces with painted eyes and special outfits were designed each year for the girl and boy dolls. This girl, with a hair wig, wears an original frock with a smocked yoke and is in particularly good condition. The dolls were marked 'Kamkins. A dolly made to love. Patented by L.R. Kampes. Atlantic City. N.J.' It is doubtful whether the interest of these dolls would be very much appreciated in the British salerooms.

£100

Fabric
Unmarked. c.1910. Height 56cm:22in.

Fabric dolls with painted features were made by J.B. Sheppard & Co. in Philadelphia from approximately 1860 to 1935 and the dolls are usually tentatively dated by their costume. This is a particularly good example in fine original condition and wearing an authentic plaid frock and underwear. It is also shown undressed so that the body construction can be seen clearly.

£200

Courtesy Beatrice L. Wright, Phoenixville, Pa.

Fabric
Marked with Chase trademarks. c.1910. Black doll 66cm:26in.

A group of dolls that were designed and made by Martha Jenks Chase in Pawtucket, Rhode Island, from 1880 to 1925. The heads were made of stockinet stretched over a mask. After coating with size, the heads and limbs were painted in oil colours. The Black Mammy Nurse was advertised in 1921 and is by far the rarest of this group. It is in fine condition and wears the original clothes. The girl, though less arresting than the nurse, has rare Dutch bobbed hair and is also seen wearing the original clothes. The redressed boy is of the most basic type with the heavily textured painted hair that is a characteristic of Chase dolls.

Black Mammy £250
Girl £120
Boy £80 – £100

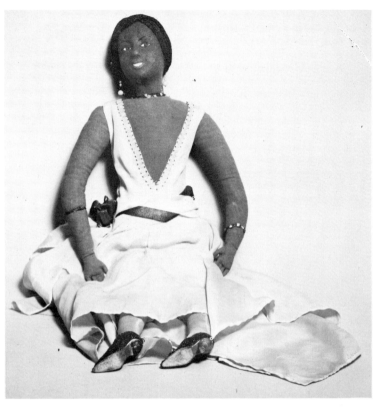

Fabric
Unmarked. c.1925. Height 65cm:25½in.

A brown cotton fabric negress with a smiling mouth and painted eyes. The head swivels within the fabric body, which is simply shaped. The original cream crêpe evening dress is worn, in this photograph back to front! The general effect of the doll is good as it is so evocative of the period.

£15 – £20

Fabric
Printed mark. c.1900. Height 44.5cm:17½in.

A printed fabric Struwwelpeter or Shockheaded Peter with long paper fingernails. The detail of the costume is printed in shades of purple and pink and the stylised rendering of the hair and face is much more dramatic than that usually seen in either American or English printed cut-out dolls of this type. The doll is marked 'Gesetzlich Geschützt. Register Number 318m. Butten & Leoning. Frankfurt a.M.' In comparison with the number printed in Britain and America, there seem to be few German dolls of this type, which gives interest to this example.

£25

BISQUE LADY DOLLS

The finest bisque lady dolls were made by the French factories and provided with the most elaborate costumes, to create miniature models of fashionable ladies of the period. Large trunks were often sold with the dolls and contained not only many changes of costume but also visiting cards, opera glasses, glove stretchers and even doll-sized sewing boxes. Despite their superb quality, many of these dolls were sold in small shops and street booths to middle class French children, as is shown in various prints of the period. A number were also exported, though to nothing like the extent of the export trade in later dolls. Marked examples, even if of poor quality, tend to fetch much higher prices than those that are unattributable. A variety of different bodies were used, the most common being of sawdust-filled gusseted leather. Those with the more unusual bodies, such as wood or gutta percha, are thus of greater interest because of rarity.

Very good quality heads are sometimes found on cheap stiff leather bodies without gussets. Dolls of this type are usually dressed in some type of regional costume and despite the quality of the heads only fetch a small percentage of the price of a more orthodox Parisienne. Black dolls of this type are very rare; men are virtually unobtainable and their price would be well above the top range given for lady dolls. The firm of Lanternier made lady dolls with composition bodies which carefully imitated the adult shape; although they are not very beautiful they are of interest as a late French version of a popular type. A great deal of a Parisienne's value depends on the originality of the clothes and their variety; reconstructions are rarely satisfactory.

Bisque lady dolls were also produced by the German porcelain factories. A few heads were mounted on leather bodies but the majority were given well-shaped bodies of composition, a few unusual examples being found with fabric bodies and composition or bisque lower arms and legs. Very few really good examples of the composition-bodied dolls of this type are seen now as they have long been popular with American collectors. They are not as startlingly impressive as the French lady dolls but still have an appeal of their own. As the original costumes of German dolls of this type were not outstanding, their presence, though desirable, is not as important as those of the Parisiennes.

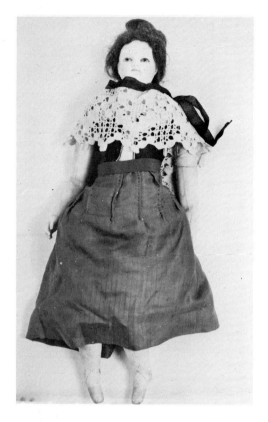

Parisienne
**Marked on body 'Aux Enfants Sages. Mme Rohmer. Joufrey, Passage
. . . Paris. c.1865. Height 43cm:17in.**

The mark makes this white bisque shoulder headed Parisienne
interesting. It has fixed blue glass eyes and a closed mouth and wears an
applied wig. The decoration of the head is very restrained, and typical
of the earlier Parisiennes. The gusseted leather body has bisque arms,
moulded to well above the elbow. Much of the original costume is lost.
The head has a very disfiguring crack across the cheek, one arm is
broken away, and the other badly cracked. The price of a doll in this
condition would be very low but for the maker's mark.

£125

Courtesy Christie's South Kensington

Parisienne
Unmarked. c.1865-1870. Height 44.5cm:17½in.

A bisque shoulder headed Parisienne with a fixed neck and the original skin wig. The head is well modelled for the type, with a rather long and pointed nose, the eyes are of blue glass. The body is in good condition and of the usual gusseted leather type, though the hands are made with more shaping than is commonly seen. The very effective original costume consists of a lilac silk dress with muslin overdress, a tatted stole, cotton stockings with red garters, high heeled cream side buttoning boots with black heels, and a charming ivory-handled parasol of black lace over a mauve silk mount. The figure is accompanied by a spare nightgown and petticoat and full underwear, including a corset. The well-made shoes are marked 'C.C'.

This is an extremely good specimen of the type, also an effective costume piece, and so commands a good price.

£800 – £900

Parisienne
Marked on body 'Mme Rohmer'. c.1865-1875. Height 39cm:15½in.

Marked Parisiennes, especially those made by a firm as desirable as Rohmer, are not common and this example, despite the fact that it has lost most of its bisque fingers, is particularly fine. Mlle. Marie Antoinette Leontine Rohmer worked in Paris between 1857 and 1880 and obtained several patents for improved methods of body articulation. This example has bright blue eyes of unusual intensity that are accentuated by a dark line painted above. The head swivels on the shoulder plate in an apparently straight line. The hair-stuffed kid body has wooden upper arms, which are hinged at the shoulders, and bisque lower arms. The kid lower legs have painted wooden-hinged knee joints. The body is stamped in an oval 'Mme Rohmer. Breveté SGDG Paris' and has two eyelet holes beneath, these holes being a particular characteristic of Rohmer's work.

£625 – £675

Parisienne
Unmarked. c.1868. Height 30.5cm:12in.

It seems highly probable that this two-faced doll was made by Leon Casimir Bru who patented several dolls, including the 'Surprise', between 1867 and 1869. 'Surprise' dolls had a concealed rod in the torso which enabled the head to turn in the bisque shoulder plate, thus revealing an alternative face. The head was presumably intended to turn under a fixed wig.

Although Bru made a large number of Parisiennes, very few were marked or boxed, but as more original catalogues are discovered some of these problems of positive attribution may be solved.

This example has a kid body and the original blue silk dress of the style worn in the 1860s when the Bru patent was first registered. The awake face is more satisfactory than the sleeping one, as the closed eyes are not painted as skilfully as might be expected.

Dolls of this type are valued almost completely on their rarity as they come on the market very infrequently and obviously every serious collector would eventually like to own an example: an ambition that can be rarely fulfilled as so few have survived.

£2,000 – £2,400

Parisienne
Unmarked. c.1870. Height 37cm:14½in.

An attractive French bisque Parisienne with a swivel neck and pierced ears. The head is well decorated and the face has rather more expression than is often seen on dolls of this type. The body is of gusseted leather and hand sewn. The complete doll is in good condition with the exception of a single missing finger.

The original commercially-made costume is in good condition and consists of a jacket and bustled skirt in cream alpaca with royal blue braid trimming and lace and silk-covered buttons. There is a matching flower trimmed hat. The doll is contained in its original but unmarked box.

£425

Souvenir Figure
Any mark would be under sewn on clothes. c.1870. Height 29cm:11½in.

The makers of bisque heads for gusseted Parisiennes also supplied the makers of costume dolls that were purchased as souvenirs. In this particular example the standard is much higher than usual, as the leather body is handsewn but without the gussets usually found on an intended Parisienne. This head is made attractive to the collector by the very large eyes.

Some dolls of this type have a very low value as part of the body is made of rather clumsy terra cotta and these are not popular with collectors. This example in its effective original costume falls somewhere between a Parisienne and a souvenir figure, and obviously if redressed by an unscrupulous person it could be passed as a more conventional Parisienne.

£130

Parisienne
Shoes marked 'T'. c.1870. Height 47cm:18½in.

A very beautiful Parisienne with a swivel neck and blue glass eyes. The original fair wig is worn but the costume is unfortunately lost and the replacement hardly flatters the doll. The white leather gusseted body is in good condition.

The shoes are marked with the letter 'T' but there were several French dollmakers whose names began with this letter and it is not possible to make a direct attribution. Other dolls, such as bébés, have been found wearing shoes marked in this way, so it is also possible that it is simply a dolls' shoemaker's mark.

£375 – £400

Parisienne
Marked '4' at hairline and shoulder. c.1870. Height 47cm:18½in.

The round-faced Parisiennes are usually of a rather earlier date than those with long and elegant features. The fact that this doll does not retain any of the original outfits is a pity, as figures of this type rely heavily on the style of costume for a close dating. The gusseted leather body is in very good general condition and is well shaped. The glass eyes are deep blue and the mouth is painted in two tones. The brows are well painted and the lashes crisply stylised. The ears are pierced. In this particular case the photograph does not reveal the beauty of the head.

£400

Courtesy Christie's South Kensington

Parisienne
Marked on shoulder '3'. c.1870. Height 46cm:18in.

An attractive bisque headed Parisienne with a swivel neck and fixed pale blue eyes. The mouth is painted in two tones for realism and the brows are well shaped. The gusseted kid body is in good condition and the original fair wig is worn. The value of the doll is enhanced by the original costume of shot grey frock decorated with fringe and buttons, and bronze coloured shoes. There are some additional garments including a tartan tea gown, two petticoats, a bridal headdress, slippers, three hair combs and earrings.

£400

Courtesy Christie's South Kensington

Parisienne
Unmarked. c.1870. Height 46cm:18in.

An extremely beautiful and quite rare doll whose value is largely lost because of its bad general state. The head is modelled to resemble a girl rather than a woman and the neck is slightly lipped. The original wig is retained and the fixed eyes are a brilliant blue. The arms are of wood with a leather covering and are ball-jointed at the elbow with the lower arms of bisque. The torso and thighs are of the usual stuffed type but from just below the thighs the body is again of jointed wood. The fingers are almost completely missing, though this would not in itself significantly affect the price. Of far more importance are the bad chips around the neck and these would be difficult to restore as the bisque is of the almost white tint that is so difficult to match perfectly, even for an expert.

£200 – £250

Courtesy Christie's South Kensington

Parisienne
Marked '2'. c.1870. Height 38cm:15in.

An unmarked Parisienne with a head of exceptionally fine quality with huge eyes and a two-tone mouth. The ears are pierced and the head swivels within the shoulder plate. One of the shoes is marked with a greyhound or some type of running dog. The body, which should be white, is unfortunately in very poor condition and much blackened which does not contribute to the effect. The original petticoat and chemise are worn. The cork pate is missing.

£275 – £300

Parisienne
Unmarked. c.1870. Height 55cm:21½in.

A Parisienne of most pleasing appearance with blue glass eyes and the original fair wig. The head is of the swivel type but there is a crack on the shoulder. A cream dress of later date is worn. The large size of this doll makes it quite impressive.

£300 – £360

Parisienne
Marked 'B Jne ET Cie' and 'E. Depose'.
1865-1870. Height 42cm:16½in.

This is not a particularly beautiful doll but is of great desirability as the head is completely marked and therefore attributable. The original cork pate is still in position though the wig is missing. The doll has fixed blue glass eyes and a two-tone smiling mouth and the body is of gusseted kid. The costume is old but of such mediocre quality that it would appear that the original fine clothes must have been lost long ago. A good price would be obtained for any doll marked by this firm even if the quality would not appear to deserve it.

£800

Parisienne
Unmarked. c.1875. Height 33cm:13in.

This interesting, though unmarked bisque swivel headed Parisienne still wears the original high buttoned boots. The head is not of particularly fine bisque and the modelling is also unexciting, but the body, with its metal upper arms, and lower arms, including the ball joints, of bisque, is very unusual. The remainder of the body is made of wood with a covering of kid, with hinge joints at the knee and thigh. Though not in exceptionally good general condition this doll has interest, though the price is lowered by the unexciting treatment of the head.

£400 – £475

Courtesy Christie's South Kensington

Parisienne
Marked on shoulder 'C' and '3'. c.1875. Height 41cm:16in.

Wooden bodied Parisiennes are among the most popular as they are without the disadvantages of gusseted leather which becomes discoloured and often assumes grotesque distorted positions. This doll's body has joints at the shoulder, elbow, wrist, thigh and knee and is in acceptable original condition. The bisque head swivels within a basic type shoulder plate and has brown eyes. Unfortunately one complete side of the head has been restored very visibly. This considerably reduces the value as a replacement head for this type of body has to be a very exact fit and might be difficult to find.

£350 – £400

Parisienne
Marked '1' on shoulder. c.1875. Height 33cm:13in.

A bisque swivel headed Parisienne with pierced ears, two-tone mouth and pale blue eyes outlined in a deep blue. The bisque is of a somewhat shiny quality and there are some slight imperfections in the paste. The gusseted kid body is hand-sewn and the toes are individually stitched. It seems likely that at some stage the head fell away from the body and was sewn back on the outside of the leather rather than with the leather being used to conceal the edge of the shoulder and the sew holes. Buyers are always a little nervous when a doll has been tampered with in this way. The straight limbed type of leather body is sometimes seen with the head crudely sewn on in a similar fashion but it is unusual on the more expensive gusseted dolls.

£235 – £245

Parisiennes
c.1870-1880. Height of standing doll 58.5cm:23in.; seated doll 56cm:22in.

The standing doll is unmarked and wears the costume of the 1880s. It is a Parisienne of the basic type, with a swivel head, bisque shoulder plate and gusseted kid body. The head is of good quality and has pale blue glass eyes with the surrounding dark lines that are associated with quality French dolls. The original blue satin dress is decorated with lace and maroon ribbons. The effect of this doll is spoiled by the grotesquely-shaped body with its monumental bust. The doll seated in the pram is marked 'F.G. 7'. This is a doll of finer quality with a more delicately decorated face and the body of more pleasing proportions. The skirt and jacket, though damaged, are original. The doll's brown shoes are marked 'Vve Schneider, St. Katherine, Anvers'.

Standing £500
Seated £450 – £500

Courtesy Sotheby's

Parisienne
Doll unmarked. c.1870-1880. Height 23cm:9in.

A good quality Parisienne reclining on a blue quilted trinket box. The beautifully modelled socketed head is mounted on a specially constructed wooden body that cannot be removed from the box. The hands are made of bisque. The original fair wig is coiled at the back of the head; the costume too, is original. The quilted box carries the label 'Boissier, 7 Boul des Capucines, Paris'. This figure would be likely to fetch a much higher price as a conventional doll rather than as a decorative box.

£400

Courtesy Christie's South Kensington

Parisienne
Marked '3' on the back of the head. c.1875.
Height 43cm:17in.

This bisque swivel headed Parisienne, with pierced ears and fixed pale blue eyes, is unusual because the shoulder plate is modelled with very definite breasts. The bisque lower arms are modelled in different positions; one is straight with the hand wide open while the other is half closed. The torso and the upper arms and legs are leather. The feet are modelled with high-heeled shoes, which have metal rimmed holes for a supporting stand. In this example one foot is damaged.

An apparently identical doll marked 'Jumeau Medaille d'or Paris', is illustrated in *The Encyclopaedia of Dolls* by D.E. and E. Coleman.

The doll wears eighteenth century style fancy dress of lilac and white satin and red woollen cape. The costume does not help the doll's appearance as it gives a rather blousy effect and fashionable clothes of the nineteenth century would be preferred.

£700 – £850

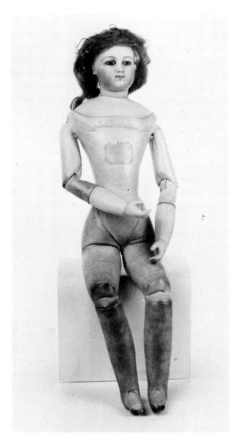

Courtesy Christie's South Kensington

Parisienne
Unmarked head. c.1875. Height 43cm:17in.

A particularly fine doll in excellent condition and carrying a 'Lavallée-Peronne' shop label on the chest. It has a swivel head and pale blue glass eyes, lined with dark blue. The decoration of this head is particularly good and the colour very subtle, the fair wig is original. The body construction, with upper arms of wood over which leather has been stretched, is more unusual. The bisque lower arms necessitated by this type of construction invariably look more attractive than arms of discoloured leather. The costume is completely missing.

£450

Parisienne
Unmarked. 1875-1885. Height 41cm:16in.

A bisque swivel headed Parisienne with pierced ears and a gusseted kid body all in good original condition. The original wig is retained and the lips are of the two-toned type. The cork pate that fits the top of the bisque head is also still in position. The quality of the bisque is not particularly fine but this is compensated for by the effective painting of the brows and the attractive modelling of the face.

The striped silk dress in shades of green is decorated with fringe and the original underwear is still worn. The dress is not very effective and is probably an old reconstruction of the original.

£300

Courtesy Christie's South Kensington

Parisienne
Marked 'B.S' and '28½?' c.1880. Height 25cm:10in.

This is an extremely difficult figure to date as the costume, though apparently original, belongs to no particular period. The quality of the head is very poor, with an almost child-like painting of the brows. Dealers and collectors used to claim that this type of crude painting was interesting as it was early and the decorators were learning their technique! In this case the cheeks are also roughly treated and the lips are very heavily coloured, altogether creating both a mean-looking and an unusually ugly doll. Heads marked in this way are sometimes attributed to Bru but this cannot at present be proven. The doll wears a pale turquoise dress and a matching hat with a flower spray. The body is of the rigid type with unshaped fingers, of the type often seen on cheap souvenir dolls. Despite its obvious shortcomings the figure does have some crude primitive appeal.

£150

Parisienne
Marked 'J' on shoes. c.1880. Height 30.5cm:12in.

Parisiennes dressed as children or young girls are only occasionally found and the original hand-sewn, but commercially produced, dress worn by this doll makes it an attractive acquisition; it would display well as part of a group of such figures. The dress is of soft blue wool. The bisque swivel head is of very fine quality and the huge eyes and skilful painting of the brows contribute to a desirable doll. It has a two-tone mouth, pierced ears and the original wig. It can be tentatively attributed to Jumeau because of their mark on the soles of the boots. The photograph does not do justice to the quality of this particular figure.

£300

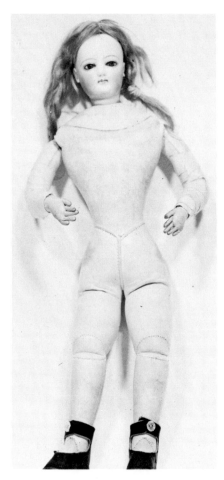

Parisienne
Marked '2' on neck and shoulder. c.1885.
Height 41cm:16in.

A bisque headed Parisienne of the more basic type with a gusseted kid body in good general condition. The eyes are pale blue, the ears are pierced, and the original fair wig is still worn. The head is quite attractive and is also in perfect condition. There are no clothes.

£300

Courtesy Phillips

Parisienne
Marked 'E'. c.1885. Height 43cm:17in.

Short velvet walking jackets of this type were popular in the mid-eighties and the fairly narrow, trainless, dress suggests the same date. The jacket is made of cut blue velvet and the skirt is cotton with braid decoration; the original underwear is worn. Though hardly a very glamorous ensemble, this costume is pleasing to the collector as it is entirely original. The body is of the usual gusseted kid construction, with a little staining, because of wear, on the separated fingers. The face, with its slight smile, is particularly beautiful as it has so much more expression than is usually found in Parisiennes. The bisque is of nice quality, the blue eyes are fixed, and the original fair wig is still worn. Though the doll is marked it is not yet possible to make any direct attribution though the presence of any tantalising indication of origin always adds interest.

£550

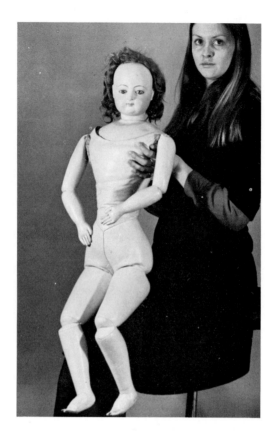

Courtesy Christie's South Kensington

Parisienne
In original box. c.1875. Height 102cm:40in.

This Parisienne, of unusually large size, is still contained in the original box labelled 'A la Ville de Caen, Margueritte Frères à Caen'. The gusseted kid body is in immaculate condition and the feet are sewn with separated toes. The colour and the quality of the bisque are acceptable and the mouth is of the two-toned type. There is a small chip on the raised neck section of the shoulder plate but as this is not too disfiguring and can be covered by a necklace it does not affect the price too considerably. It is the sheer size of this doll rather than any quality of manufacture that makes it desirable.

£1,300

Bisque Lady
Unmarked. c.1910. Height 52cm:20½in.

A bisque shoulder headed lady doll with a particularly well modelled face. These heads were made in smaller numbers than the more common waxed compositions of this style. Lady dolls enjoyed a fresh burst of popularity in the years before the First World War but were made at that time in Germany rather than France, and were of a cheaper construction than their forerunners, the Parisiennes. The quality of the bisque is excellent and the expression is pleasing with the added interest of an open-closed mouth. The body is of the very cheap type usually associated with the most inexpensive waxed and composition dolls and has painted black shoes. The lower arms and legs are composition. Much of the value of this doll lies in the superb costume of elaborate court dress with pink satin train trimmed with flower sprays and lace. Accessories include finely made miniature kid gloves, fan and nightgown. The clothes are sewn in position so the doll was probably intended for display rather than play. Similar dolls are found stamped with the green numbers usually associated with Gebruder Heubach and the combination of good quality head with poor body is also typical of this manufacturer.

£300

Courtesy Christie's South Kensington

Parisienne
Marked '4 FG 4'. c.1870. Height 41cm:16in.

It is extremely difficult to evaluate an assembled doll, such as this with its stuffed fabric body and wooden arms. The head is, of course, a good quality marked Parisienne's, probably made by Fernand Gaultier, with fixed deep blue eyes. The value is, however, considerably enhanced by a number of spare clothes and accessories. It is sometimes possible to find a more appropriate body for such a doll, so that a price higher than might be expected is sometimes achieved. The estimated value, therefore, is for the made up doll alone, and in its present condition.

£140 – £150

German Bisque
Marked '1469 Simon and Halbig 2'. c.1916
Height 37cm:14½in.

The Simon and Halbig lady dolls are almost invariably attractive, as they are so delicately constructed, despite the fact that the bodies are of the double jointed type. The original costume of this doll consisting of a pink silk frock printed with chiné roses, stockings and nicely made brown leather high-heeled shoes makes it a particularly desirable acquisition. The head is modelled with a closed mouth and blue sleeping eyes. The modelling is delicate but the colour is very high, which seems typical of dolls made in this mould. This heavy colour is, however, outweighed by the presence of the charming costume and the perfect general condition of the figure.

£250

German Bisque
Marked '1159 Simon and Halbig 8 S&H'. c.1920.
Height 53cm:21in.

Simon and Halbig dolls of the open-mouthed type with bodies modelled as women are nothing like as popular as those with the much sweeter closed-mouth modelling. Wearing magenta silk pyjamas and with the brown hair piled on the head, this figure comes with the original green-lined wardrobe containing clothes including a flower-embroidered muslin frock. Though the dress as seen in the picture forms an interesting costume document of the period, it does not enhance the appearance for the general doll buyer.

£190 – £200

German Bisque
Marked '1469 S&H 2'. c.1912. Height 41cm:16in.

A Simon and Halbig lady doll with closed mouth and pierced ears. The eyes are of the sleeping type with very small eyelashes. The original long, fair mohair wig is worn, held back by a large black taffeta bow. The navy blue and white silk outfit is also original though the fabric, as in so many of the factory-dressed dolls of this type, is splitting along the folds. The black silk stockings, ending just above the knees, and the leather heeled shoes are also factory-made. The body is of the usual slender type with a shaped bust and the original wire stringing is still intact; this is a definite advantage, as dolls of this delicate construction are often difficult to restring, to exactly the right tension, with elastic. It is contained in the original box with a small embroidered pillow. The box is marked 'Made in Germany Dz. No. Special H' with a coat of arms beneath.

£250

GERMAN BISQUE HEADED DOLLS

So great was the production of bisque headed dolls in Germany that the French industry declined, since any real competition was impossible. There were hundreds of German factories, most of which obligingly incised their trademarks on the dolls' heads, so that attribution is usually possible, though there are still many marks that have not yet been traced to the makers. The German doll was made in two basic types: one has a bisque shoulder head mounted on a leather or fabric body while the other has a head of the socket type and a jointed composition body. The kid bodied dolls are always popular as they have a look of a good quality hand-assembled object, those with closed mouths and made by such firms as Simon and Halbig being the most popular. The quality of the majority of the socket heads is generally of a good standard, especially when the vast number produced is considered. These heads usually have sleeping eyes lead weighted for movement, and open mouths with inserted teeth; in some of the better examples the teeth are moulded, as in French dolls. The price of some of the fairly ordinary German dolls rose startlingly during 1977 due to the great increase in the number of new collectors in Germany, Holland and Japan. At the time of writing they appear overpriced in relation to much rarer dolls and it will be interesting to see if this new price level will be maintained, as it has been in relation to wax dolls.

At the beginning of the twentieth century there was great interest in the modelling of dolls' heads which resembled real children and the so called 'character heads' were made. In quantity, they never competed with the doll-faced dolls and therefore have a value based entirely on rarity. Some models, such as the Kammer and Reinhardt 126, appear very regularly and consequently command a price that is only a little above that possible for an ordinary baby doll, while others, such as the 114, can easily fetch over £600. Generally the American market is better supplied with character dolls than the European, as the great majority were exported to the States when new. Some character dolls therefore fetch prices in England which American collectors consider highly inflated.

The German makers produced a much greater variety of dolls than the French including Indian, negro, Chinese and Polynesian. Some were even made with the frightening wrinkled faces of witches. All these dolls have a value that is dependent on rarity. The more amusing variations, such as the two-faced dolls, remain constantly popular though in real terms they have suffered a slight price drop recently.

The greatest share of the German market was taken by the firm of Armand Marseille and a very high percentage of all the old dolls found was made by this factory. In their case value is purely dependent upon quality as heads from the same basic model vary greatly.

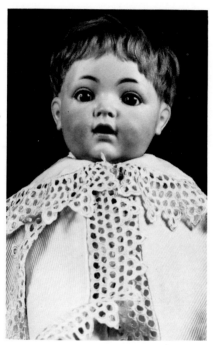

Courtesy Christie's South Kensington

German Bisque
Marked 'K&R Simon and Halbig 121 50'. c.1920. Height 47cm:18½in.

A bisque headed German doll made for Kammer and Reinhardt by the porcelain factory of Simon and Halbig. It has a bent limb baby body and is dressed in baby robes and a carrying cape. This doll was also made as a jointed doll with a toddler type body, a version that is better liked than the baby type. This has blue sleeping eyes and an open mouth. The brows are well painted. A type of doll that is more popular in the States than in Europe. As the centimetre size given in the mark (50) does not correspond to the actual height, this doll would appear to be on the wrong body, and the price is reduced accordingly.

£175

German Bisque
Unmarked. c.1880. Height approx. 51cm:20in.

The closed mouth German shoulder headed dolls of this period have a peculiarly haunting charm. The faces are very beautiful and the dolls have more general appeal even than the French ones, which are so collectable, but whose expression is a rather cultivated taste. In this example, with sleeping blue glass eyes, the head is turned to the right. The colouring is effective and the general condition is good. The cloth body has bisque lower arms and the lower legs are of the type usually associated with the 'blonde bisque' type of doll as they have moulded boots which give a rather disconcerting effect. They are not necessarily replacements, as these early German heads are often seen on completely original bodies which are not of the type we automatically associate with later versions. An example in the author's collection, for instance, has arms that at first glance appear much too small for the size of the doll but on examination are found to be completely authentic to the figure.

This doll wears the original cream silk dress and cream felt flannel cape trimmed with imitation fur, and there is also some spare clothing and a bonnet.

£300 – £325

Courtesy Christie's South Kensington

German Bisque
Unmarked. c.1885. Height 46cm:18in.

An attractive German bisque shoulder headed girl doll with the head turned very sharply to the right. The modelling is heavy and the expression effective. The fixed eyes are brown and a long brown hair wig is worn. The original body, of the best quality German type such as that used on some early Simon and Halbigs, is pink and gusseted, with the lower arms made of bisque. The proportions of the doll are not entirely satisfactory as the arms seem overlong and the head overlarge for the total height though it is completely original. The adult style evening dress does little for the appearance as these dolls were originally made as German competitors for bébés such as those made by Bru and would be more suitably dressed in girls' clothes.

£300 – £350

German Bisque
Marked 'S&H 1079 DEP'. c.1900. Height 74cm:29in.

A very large Simon and Halbig with fixed brown eyes, heavy brows, and the original mohair wig. The mouth is modelled open with moulded teeth. The colour of the bisque is a little strong but it is not unpleasant. The body, which is also in good condition, is of the heavy rather thick limbed type representing a toddler. A red velvet frock and a white embroidered pinafore are worn with a child's bonnet and old shoes. These large Simon and Halbigs have reached some quite surprising sums at auctions over the last two years, prices often not supported by any high standard of finish but purely based on size.

£185 – £200

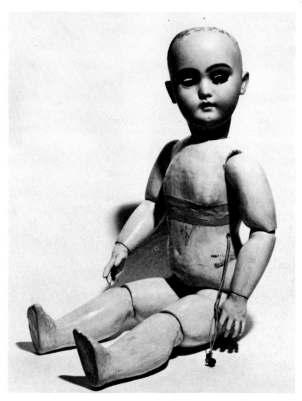

German Bisque
Marked on head and body. c.1905. Height 52cm:20½in.

A Simon and Halbig sleeping-eyed doll with the head marked 'S&H 1079 DEP. Germany' and stamped 'Wimpern. Gesetze Geschutz'. This is one of the better Simon and Halbig heads and the Wimpern mark seems frequently to be found on dolls of this make which were intended for the French market. The body, with two pull strings to activate the simple voice box, is marked 'Bébé Le Parisien. Medaille d'Or Paris' a mark used by the Steiner company. It is accepted that Simon and Halbig supplied heads to the Jumeau factory but such a head mounted on a Steiner body is obviously distrusted despite the excellent matching of the neck to the body socket.

£90 – £100

German Bisque
Marked 'S H 1199 Germany DEP 3½'. c.1900. Height 30.5cm:12in.

Oriental jointed girl dolls have appeared regularly at auction recently after a few strikingly high prices were obtained and it would seem very likely that a downward curve in the price will be seen as the dolls are not uncommon though most collectors like to include at least one in their display. This has a yellow tinted composition body and wears the original costume.

£400

German Bisque
Marked 'S&H 1129 dep 6½'. c.1900. Height 36cm:14in.

A jointed bisque headed doll modelled as a Japanese girl and made by
Simon and Halbig. The body is tinted yellow. The black wool wig is
held by a comb and the ears are pierced. The mouth is slightly open to
reveal the teeth. Although the head is attractive it is not as perfect in
appeal as that of the following larger example and would be expected
to fetch a lower price both because of its smaller size and because of its
remade costume.

£400

Courtesy Christie's South Kensington

German Bisque
Marked '8 Simon and Halbig'. c.1900. Height 48cm:19in.

A particularly fine quality bisque headed doll modelled to represent a Japanese girl with slanting almond shaped brown sleeping eyes. The colouring of the head is very realistic and the jointed body is of a matching light ochre colour. The wig is original as are the shoes and jacket. The ears are pierced. Only infrequently does such a fine quality example occur and this quality is reflected in the price. Other dolls by the same firm and even cast from the same model do not have this magic.

£500

German Bisque
Marked '1329 Simon & Halbig S&H 2'. c.1900. Height 33cm:13in.

This was the last Simon and Halbig jointed oriental doll to appear at auction in the period on which this price guide is based and is remarkable in that it confirms the lower price trend, seen over several sales, for this model. This example is well coloured and in good condition. As the dolls are not rare they were obviously becoming overpriced and are now going somewhat out of fashion among collectors who usually wish to acquire only one example.

£350

Courtesy Phillips

German Bisque
Marked 'Simon & Halbig S&H4'. c.1920. Height 33cm:13in.

An unusually dark Simon and Halbig with slightly negroid features, brown sleeping eyes, the mouth modelled in an open position with teeth and the ears pierced. The body is of the good quality found on many Simon and Halbig examples with turned wooden arms, while the body colour matches the head colour unusually well — frequently a weak point on dolls of the coloured type. The original white cotton embroidered frock is worn with a yellow muslin apron. The underwear is also in good condition.

£200 – £225

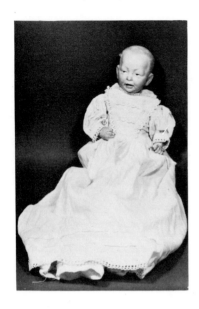

German Bisque
Marked '28 K&R 100'. c.1910. Height 27cm:10½in.

Kammer and Reinhardt introduced a completely new concept in the modelling of the heads of bisque dolls when they created their character baby doll that was known by the firm as 'Baby'. Collectors once believed that the head was modelled on the young son of the German monarch and it was known for many years as the 'Kaiser Baby', a term still sometimes used as an easy means of identification, though it is now generally known that it was in fact modelled from the sculptor's son.

This doll has the usual slightly moulded, painted hair and an open-closed mouth. The eyes are also painted and the body is made with one arm bent into a much higher position than the other so that the doll could assume a crawling stance. A replacement body, even if of the same period, would almost halve the value though it should be remembered that early versions of this head were sometimes originally mounted on jointed bodies which are, of course, acceptable. As most collectors want an example of a doll that was so important in the development of their subject, 'Baby' usually fetches a reasonable price though it has not appreciated as much in value over the last ten years as the basic dolly faced bisques.

£200

German Bisque
Marked '28 P* A 100'. c.1911. Height 27cm:10½in.

A bisque headed character baby obviously made in imitation of the character doll made by Kammer and Reinhardt and marked '100', though as yet this mark is unattributable. The head is effectively modelled with painted eyes and the appearance is further enhanced by the original white frock trimmed with ribbon and lace. The body, made of composition, is of the bent limb type.

£140 – £160

German Bisque
Marked '309-2'. c.1885. Height 56cm:22in.

A bisque shoulder headed girl doll with sleeping blue eyes and an open mouth; the body of the basic leather type used by several makers has composition lower arms and lower legs. There is some restoration to the hands but this is fairly well done and does not detract from the price. A crocheted frock, with a hanging pocket, and hat are worn. The dress originally had a short train but has shrunk in washing so the train now only reaches calf level.

£130 – £150.

Courtesy Phillips

German Bisque
Marked 'K&R 114'. Early 20th century. Height 48cm:19in.

Another good example of the pouting '114' made by Kammer and Reinhardt. Both the head and the jointed body are in good condition.

£900 – £950

German Bisque
Marked 'K&R 101'. c.1910. Height 41cm:16in.

After the introduction of 'Baby', number 100, by Kammer and Reinhardt in 1909, other character dolls were created though they were never in such great demand. The '101' was assembled either as a boy or girl doll and named Peter or Marie by the firm itself. This example has painted sideways glancing eyes but a few very rare examples are known with sleeping eyes. It was thought when the dolls were made that their lack of popularity with the toy trade was because they were not given sleeping eyes; an insertion that was difficult because of the realistic modelling of the face. In fact those with the painted eyes are artistically much more beautiful but the rarity of the sleeping-eyed version would command an even higher figure. This good example has blue eyes and is made of very good quality bisque with fairly soft colouring. The jointed body is also in nice condition.

£700 – £800

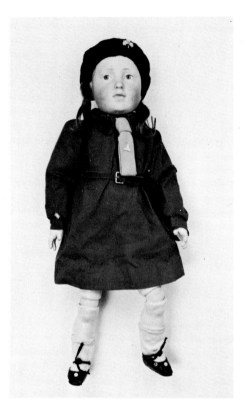

German Bisque
Marked 'K&R 109 43'. c.1912. Height 42cm:16½in.

A closed mouth character girl made by Kammer and Reinhardt and known as Elsie. It has the characteristic brown painted eyes, and the wistful expression of a moment on a child's face is skilfully caught by the modeller. The double jointed composition body is dressed in a Girl Guide uniform. This doll is rarer than the '114' and should command a substantial price.

£950

Courtesy Christie's South Kensington

German Bisque
Marked 'K&R 100'. c.1912. Height 48cm:19in.

A particularly good example of the Kammer and Reinhardt 'Baby' with well tinted bisque and crisply defined features. The doll has the usual painted blue eyes and open-closed mouth. It is dressed in a cream silk robe.

£200

Courtesy Phillips

Courtesy Phillips

German Bisque
Marked 'K&R 114'. Early 20th century. Height 42cm:16½in.

Kammer and Reinhardt of Waltershausen were the first company to introduce character heads and by 1910 Hans and Gretchen (114), were being made. The illustrated doll with a long mohair wig is Gretchen. Although the dolls were very appealing, they were produced for a relatively short period and are no longer seen in the catalogues of the 1920s.

This example has blue painted eyes and a very firmly closed, rather sulky, mouth. Note the painted highlights to the eyes and the very rudimentary painting of the brows that would be considered poor on any doll other than a character. The double jointed body is in need of some attention and two fingers are missing. In examples of some scarcity value, minor damage such as this becomes less relevant as long as the bisque head is perfect.

Despite the fact that the costume is original it is in poor general condition though very restorable.

£800 – £850

German Bisque
Marked 'K&R 109'. c.1912. Height 38cm:15in.

The Kammer and Reinhardt character girl known as Elsie is rarer than the '114' so that even an example as obviously cracked as this can still be expected to fetch a substantial price. The modeller has skilfully caught the fleeting expression on a child's face. The painted brown eyes, with a heavy dark line suggesting the lid, look very slightly sideways and the cheeks are delicately dimpled. A replacement mohair wig is worn and the body is in extremely good condition. A contemporary brown, orange and yellow printed cotton dress is worn.

£350 – £400

Courtesy Christie's South Kensington

German Bisque
Marked 'Simon and Halbig K&R 90'. c.1905. Height 91.5cm:36in.

A fairly basic Kammer and Reinhardt jointed girl doll only made unusual by its very large size. Very big dolls are often popular with new collectors though the more established find their display a problem. Occasionally a private museum or a decorator will pay an unusually high sum for large dolls purely for use in display. This doll, wearing its original broderie anglaise frock, brown leather shoes and plum velvet coat, also has additional items including a bonnet and some pieces of jewellery. It is contained in a large and rather coffin-like cloth covered box. It has an open mouth and blue sleeping eyes.

£250

Courtesy Sotheby's

German Bisque
Marked 'K star R'. c.1925. Height 47cm:18½in.

A Kammer and Reinhardt bisque socket-headed doll with a jointed composition body, sleeping blue eyes and an open mouth. The cheek is a little rubbed, which detracts from the value. This is not among the more effective K&R heads but the original costume is quite attractive.

£85

German Bisque
Marked 'K star R Simon and Halbig 116A'. c.1920. Height 63.5cm:25in.

A bisque headed character baby doll made extremely attractive by the original blue linen Norfolk jacket with matching trousers and embroidered decoration. It has a typical bent limb baby body. The head has blue sleeping eyes, an open-closed mouth with two painted teeth and is modelled with a pleasing alert expression.

£200

German Bisque
Marked 'K&R 117 76'. c.1912. Height 77.5cm:30½in.

An unusually large Simon and Halbig doll made to the specifications of Kammer and Reinhardt with the usual good quality jointed body common to K&R. The head, which is in perfect condition, is of the closed mouth type and the blue eyes sleep. The doll still wears its original factory wig in light brown mohair. The colour of the bisque is good and the quality typical of better K&Rs. Dolls of this type are at present at an unusually high popularity peak and such a large example would command a high price.

£850 – £1,000

Courtesy Sotheby's

German Bisque
Marked 'Heinrich Handwerck'. c.1885. Height 46cm:18in.

Heinrich Handwerck was producing dolls from Waltershausen as early as 1876 and registered several patents for body improvements. Several of his dolls were given names intended to appeal to the French market and their quality is usually good. This strongly modelled example wears the original grey alpaca bonnet and dress with pink stitching and has the original mohair wig. The brows are heavy and the doll has sleeping brown eyes and an open mouth. The general condition is good but there is a tiny chip over one eye.

£80 – £85

Courtesy Christie's South Kensington

German Bisque
Marked 'C.O.D. 23- 1 DEP'. c.1885. Height 48cm:19in.

The impressed marks on the shoulder head make this bisque doll attributable to the firm of Cuno and Otto Dressel of Sonneberg. The jointed kid body has bisque lower arms, sleeping blue eyes, and the original auburn wig. The colouring on almost all the C.O.D. dolls of this type is very pale and the shaping is quite delicate. The original apricot coloured dress and hat are worn with a velvet bolero. Not an unusual doll, but a good example of its type and therefore of interest to a collector who might want to represent the factory.

£100 – £125

German Bisque
Marked 'Jutta 1914 5½'. c.1914. Height 35.5cm:14in.

A bent limbed baby that was probably made originally at the date suggested by the mark on the head. The trade mark Jutta was registered by Cuno and Otto Dressel. This doll is appealing because of its very complete costume, all made of lace-trimmed cream silk. The original mohair wig is worn and the colour of the bisque is rather high. The sleeping eyes are of an unusual pale blue and the teeth are of the fine quality seen on Kammer and Reinhardt dolls, probably due to the fact that Simon and Halbig made heads both for K&R and for Cuno and Otto Dressel.

£80

German Bisque
Marked 'Heinrich Handwerck Simon and Halbig 8'.

c.1910. Height 91cm:36in.

A doll which depends almost completely for its value on its very large size as the face is rather highly coloured for popular taste. As with the majority of dolls made by Simon and Halbig the bisque is of good quality. The modelling of the face, to the Handwerck specification, is typical of the 'dolly faced' era in the early twentieth century. The Handwerck firm was apparently taken over by Kammer and Reinhardt in 1902, after Heinrich's death. This doll has brown sleeping eyes and pierced ears. The body, in good condition, is double jointed. The original mohair wig is worn and a contemporary embroidered silk smock. Very large figures of this type are liked as they do create an effective display.

£250 – £275

German Bisque
Marked 'S&H'. Early 20th century. Height 38cm:15in.

A Simon and Halbig Burmese girl in the original costume, which is in extremely good condition, and still wearing the original black mohair wig. The colouring of the head is good and the body is also both well tinted and in fine condition.

The double-jointed oriental type Simon and Halbigs have been enjoying a burst of popularity. Over the last two years prices have ranged from £280 in March 1976 to £750 in December of the same year. These dolls are at present dropping in price as more examples appear and they may be expected to stabilise around the quoted figure.

£450

Courtesy Phillips

German Bisque
Marked under wig. 1914-1918. Height 29cm:11½in.

It is the effectively made original costume that provides the especial interest in this fairly small German doll. It represents the uniform worn by soldiers in the First World War, though the rather elegant shoes might have been rather out of place in the trenches. The body is of the straight limbed type and the head is pale in colour and of such fine bisque that it is probably the work of Simon and Halbig. The doll has brown sleeping eyes and the original mohair wig.

£75 – £85

Courtesy Christie's South Kensington

German Bisque
Marked '79' with Heubach sunburst and '4'. Early 20th century.
Height 20cm: 8in.

Gebrüder Heubach made an almost astonishing range of character heads, the majority of which are modelled with sympathy for the subject, be it a sulking child or a whistling boy. These heads are often mounted on bodies of very indifferent quality. Though bonnets moulded in one with the head are not uncommon in conjunction with a moulded shoulder head, they are rare on the later socket heads, which is why this doll is always popular; it has been given the name of 'Baby Stuart' by collectors. The most desirable version of this head has a bonnet that actually lifts off, but any are worthwhile acquisitions. Here, the bisque bonnet is moulded in position and is decorated with transfer printed flowers. At the front corners of the bonnet are small holes through which ribbon was originally threaded to 'tie' it. The head has intaglio eyes and a closed mouth. The toddler type composition body is generally in a state of poor repair.

£275

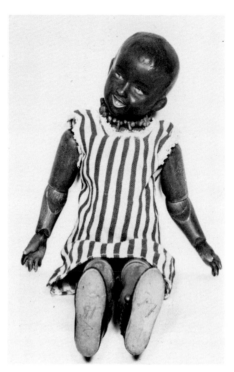

Courtesy Christie's South Kensington

German Bisque
**Marked with Heubach sunburst '76 DEP 04 2/0'. c.1920.
Height 28cm:11in.**

This photograph hardly does justice to the clever modelling of this dark brown character head made by Heubach. The short, slightly ruffled hair is moulded and the eyes are of the brown intaglio type; the open-closed mouth has two lower teeth. The body is of unusually good quality for this firm who often used very cheap composition. This, of carved wood and composition, is much more typical of the work of Simon and Halbig. The original brown shoes and red and white striped shirt with a coral necklace are worn. These coloured Heubach characters are some of the most effective that the firm produced.

£300

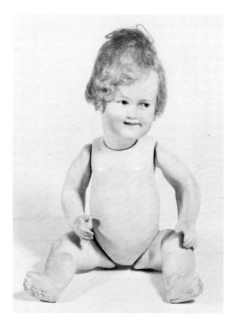

German Bisque
Marked with square Heubach mark. c.1912. Height 23cm:9in.

A good quality bisque headed character child with a socket head mounted on a composition bent limb body that is well made for a firm often associated with bodies of poor construction. The painted features are very well defined and the teeth in the open-closed mouth are well painted. The intaglio eyes glance sharply to the left. A particularly good example.

£200 – £225

Courtesy Christie's South Kensington

German Bisque
Marked 'O' with a sunburst. Height 29cm:11½in.

Heubach heads of very acceptable quality are frequently found on very cheaply made bodies, though this example is even worse than usual and a replacement would be needed to make the figure saleable from a shop. The shoulder head has the characteristic Heubach intaglio eyes and short moulded hair. The mouth is closed. The shoulder headed version of this doll is not as common as the socket type.

£125

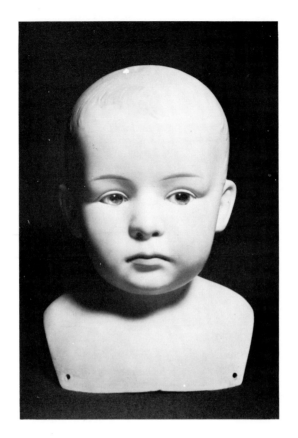

German Bisque
Marked with square Heubach mark. c.1912. Height 23cm:9in.

Very large Gebrüder Heubach shoulder heads of this type are only found occasionally and this example is strikingly fine with its effective modelling and charming sulky expression, seen also in many dolls of their socket headed type. The eyes are of the usual intaglio type with highlights. If a suitable body could be found for it this doll would be unusually large and very highly collectable.

£250

Antiques of Childhood, Camden Passage

German Bisque
Marked with an impressed size 'O Germany' and a green printed '56'.
1905. Height 28cm:11in.

Gebrüder Heubach made these pensive faced character babies in very large numbers and in a wide variety of sizes but they have such appealing faces that a good price is always reached, despite the fact that they are quite common. This baby, with a socket head, has the typical Heubach intaglio eyes and lightly moulded hair. The bent limbed body is of a heavy quality composition. It wears a black velvet lace trimmed suit.

£120

German Bisque
Marked ' "9578? 2 Heubach'. Early 20th century. Height 20cm:8in.

Dolls with their eye sockets cut in an accentuated round manner are known to collectors as googlies and have become extremely popular during the 1970s. In this Heubach example the eyes glance to the right and the smiling mouth is closed. The composition baby's body wears a chemise. A good pale bisque and an attractive head, though the eyes are not sufficiently exaggerated to satisfy the collectors of the most amusing dolls of the type.

£220 – £250

German Bisque
Marked 'Revalo 3 DEP'. c.1920. Height 25cm:10in.

Bisque headed dolls marked Revalo were made by Gebrüder Heubach for Gebrüder Ohlhaver. The Heubach character dolls are a popular collecting field and most collectors like to own an example. The moulded hair is coloured a soft brown and is held by a moulded pink ribbon with additional pink rosettes above the ears. The mouth is open-closed and the intaglio eyes are painted grey. The body is of the bent limb type.

£175

German Bisque
Marked 'Revalo 3 DEP'. c.1920. Height 27cm:10½in.

Another example of a Revalo doll, but this time with a blue, not pink, band in the hair. The hair is pale brown, the eyes are intaglio and the open-closed mouth reveals the teeth. The body is composition and is dressed in a rather unflattering crochet dress. The unpredictable way in which current prices are moving is indicated by prices achieved for this and the previous doll of almost identical quality, the former reaching £300 at auction and this, a few months later, £200.

£175 – £200

German Bisque
Marked 'A.M 370'. c.1900. Height 41cm:16in.

The value of even a fairly basic doll is considerably increased if that doll is provided with several changes of well-made clothes. This shoulder headed doll has a leather body and composition lower legs and arms. The tinting of the head is reasonably soft and the general condition of the whole figure is good. It has brown sleeping eyes and an open mouth with teeth. The costume, of white embroidered frock and lace trimmed bonnet, is effective and there are also pink fabric shoes trimmed with rosettes. The doll has the original fair wig.

£150

Courtesy Antiques of Childhood, Camden Passage

German Bisque
Marked 'A 3 M 390 Germany'. c.1905. Height 46cm:18in.

A basic Armand Marseille doll with a double jointed body and a bisque socket head, made a little more interesting because the original white muslin dress is still worn. The doll wears a hair wig that is a replacement. Many of the original mohair wigs used by this firm were so mean that it is now difficult to sell a doll that still wears the original cheaper kind of wig. This doll has an open mouth, two teeth and blue sleeping eyes.

£85

German Bisque
Marked 'Made in Germany. Armand Marseille 390.D.R.G.M. 246/1 A.5.M'.
1905. Height 56cm:22in.

Despite the fact that the same basic model was used, the Armand
Marseille 390, the most commonly found of jointed dolls, is found with
a variety of expressions, from those with huge eyes and superb bisque
to others with small mean eyes and imperfect bisque. This example has
the unjointed wrists that collectors tend to associate with the earlier
examples of the type, and a jointed body. The open mouth contains
four teeth and the very dark blue eyes contribute to the rather unusual
expression. The doll wears a reconstructed blue silk dress and a muslin
pinafore.

£85 – £90

Courtesy Christie's South Kensington

German Bisque
Marked 'A.M 341'. c.1920. Height 28cm:11in.

Two nicely matched Armand Marseille closed mouth babies with flange necks mounted on stuffed bodies with squeakers. Both have the original celluloid hands and are identically dressed in white robes with blue herring-bone embroidery. One doll has blue eyes and the other brown. The matched pair make an amusing combination, so the price is higher than for two small single dolls of this type.

£120

Courtesy Sotheby's

German Bisque
**Marked 'A.M. 560 A2M DRMR232 Made in Germany'. c.1925.
Height 41cm:16in.**

An Armand Marseille character doll with grey sleeping eyes and an open mouth. The body is of the usual jointed type and a later checked frock is worn. Though the head is of interest, the doll is spoiled by the very unpleasant dark red that was used for the lips and consequently the doll commands only a comparatively low figure.

£90

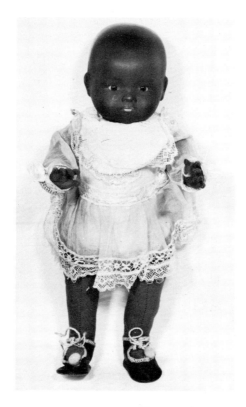

German Bisque
Marked '341/2'. c.1925. Height 30.5cm:12in.

A baby doll with a brown flange-necked head mounted on a brown cotton body of the straight legged type and with the original celluloid hands. The original muslin frock with a bib and pearl bracelet is also worn. The eyes are of the brown sleeping type. Though the general effect of this doll, in its charming outfit, is good, it is somewhat marred by the very unsympathetic painting of the lips in a harsh colour and the texture of the fired-on colour which is very thick. More delicate finishing is preferred. For some reason, dolls of this type, although they are not uncommon, have recently fetched considerably more in the London auction rooms than when sold by dealers.

£90 – £100

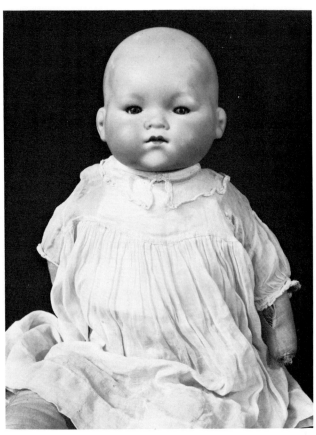

Courtesy Phillips

German Bisque
Marked 'A.M. Germany'. c.1920. Height 60cm:23½in.

A large flange necked Dream Baby of attractively coloured bisque. It has blue eyes of the sleeping type and a closed mouth. The head is mounted on a stuffed fabric body though the composition or celluloid hands are missing. This does not detract too heavily from the value as replacement hands can be obtained from several commercial suppliers of dolls' parts. The untidy and recent baby dress does not help the general effect but sympathetically redressed this would be an appealing doll.

£85

German Bisque
Marked 'A.M. Germany. 513 O½ K'. c.1930. Height 32cm:12½in.

A bent limbed baby doll with a painted bisque head, sleeping glass eyes and two teeth. The painted bisques photograph well and appear attractive but, in fact, the painted colour becomes very easily rubbed and there are frequently imperfections. Baby dolls of this type continued to be made until just before the last war.

£40

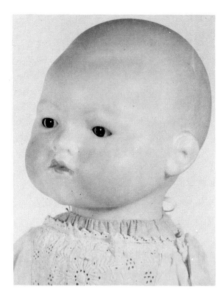

Courtesy Christie's South Kensington

Courtesy Phillips

German Bisque
Marked 'A.M 341/8'. c.1920. Height 53cm:21in.

A very good example of the Armand Marseille closed mouth baby. The bisque is a good colour and of nice quality and the eyes are well aligned. The flange head is mounted on the original stuffed fabric body with celluloid hands. A white embroidered gown is worn.

£90 – £100

German Bisque
Marked 'A 2/0 M. D.R.G.M.'. Early 20th century. Height 25cm:10in.

The character dolls that were introduced in the early twentieth century by K&R were soon copied by other firms though they never became as popular with children of the period as the basic sweet-faced playthings. Consequently they survive in a far lower number and even examples whose bisque is poor and whose decoration is mediocre can fetch reasonable prices. This example was made by Armand Marseille and is attractive as it still retains its original costume which, despite the rather rough construction, is effective. Few dolls still retain their original wigs and this mohair version is plaited into the 'earphones' that was a popular German style of the period.

The head, with its blue painted eyes and closed mouth with accompanying dimples, has some appeal despite the mediocre quality of the bisque. The condition of the body is virtually mint.

£140

German Bisque
Marked 'A.M.S/O'. c.1910. Height 20cm:8in.

A bisque headed doll made by Armand Marseille and modelled to represent an Indian with a furrowed brow. The brown eyes are fixed but not very well fitting in this small example. These Indian heads vary quite considerably in quality and this is one of the poorer, though the good condition of the original costume is a great advantage.

£80

German Bisque
Marked 'Made in Germany. A 4 M'. c.1914. Height 37cm:14½in.

A most attractive character child made by Armand Marseille. It has a very effective drooping closed mouth which creates the impression that the doll is at any moment going to burst into tears. The eyes are blue painted intaglio and a good fair mohair wig is worn. This doll illustrates the fact that although Armand Marseille dolls are very common, their rare characters are highly desirable.

£750

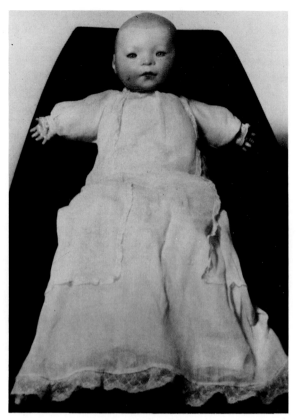

Courtesy Beatrice L. Wright, Phoenixville, Pa.

German Bisque
Marked 'L.A.&S. 1914' with copyright. c.1914.
Height approx. 51cm:20in.

This American designed doll with a bisque head especially made in Germany represents an idealised two day old infant. It was designed from life by Jeno Juszko and made by Louis Amberg & Son. The copyright number, which was registered by Amberg 'G. 45520' is found on many of the heads. This example has a cloth body and composition hands but these dolls were also made with composition heads. It is a much more appealing doll than the Bye-lo and designed much earlier, yet it is not as widely known. It was named the 'New Born Babe'.

£175

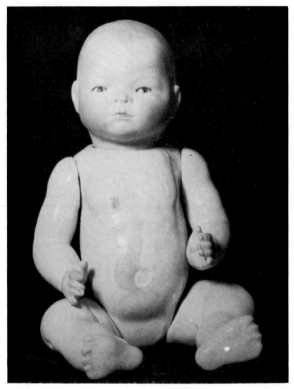

Courtesy Beatrice L. Wright, Phoenixville, Pa.

German Bisque
Marked 'Cpr. 1923 by Grace S. Putnam.' c.1922.
Circumference of head 30.5cm:12in.

A Bye-Lo Baby with a composition body and unusual socket neck. The 1922 copyright described a 'neck constructed to fit a socket' but the design was soon changed and the soft body is more usual. Both the socket type and the flange necked heads were sold separately, presumably for home assembly. This example on a commercially made body has the usual sleeping eyes and closed mouth and is in perfect condition. It is doubtful whether the rarity of the head would be appreciated by many Europeans.

£100 – £130

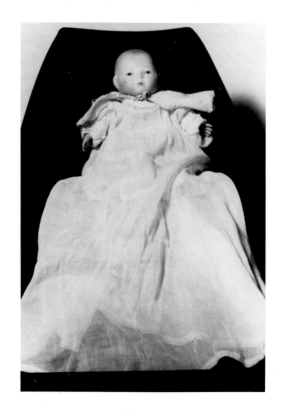

Courtesy Beatrice L. Wright, Phoenixville, Pa.

German Bisque
Marked 'Cr 1923 Grace S Putnam. Made in Germany' c.1925.
Circumference of head 36cm:14in.

A good example of a Bye-Lo Baby designed by Grace Storey Putman and modelled on the head of an actual baby. It was made in bisque to the specifications of the Borgfeldt company of New York who also organised the distribution. The heads were made in bisque by several German factories including Kling, Kestner and Alt, Beck & Gottschalck. The flange necked heads were attached to soft bodies with celluloid hands by the K&K Toy Company in the States. These dolls were not exported in any quantity and often fetch higher prices in Europe because of scarcity.

£150 – £200

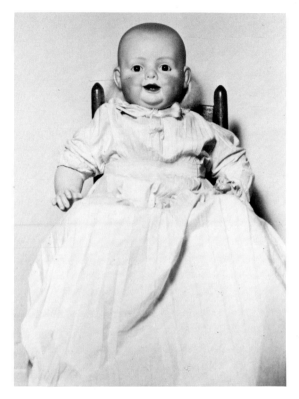

German Bisque
Marked. 1923-26. Height approx. 46cm:18in.

This bisque headed doll is known to American collectors as 'Bonnie Babe' or 'Georgene Averill Baby'. It has a realistic character head and was designed by Madam Georgene Averill, who also used the trade name of Madam Hendren. Her husband, Paul Averill, ran the Averill Manufacturing Company which produced dolls. Alt, Beck & Gottschalck produced some of the bisque heads for Bonnie Babe.

£185 – £200

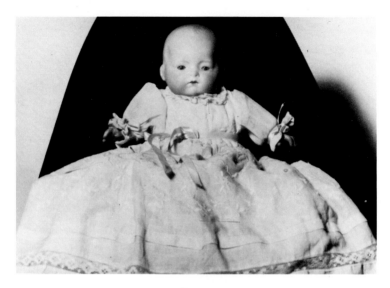

German Bisque
Marked 'Germany ARRANBEE'. c.1925. Height approx. 41cm:16in.

The Arranbee Doll Company of New York imported dolls' heads and hospital supplies from Germany and was also a doll assembler. 'My Dream Baby' was registered as a trademark by this company in 1925, the doll being made by Armand Marseille. The Arranbee dolls are of much greater interest to American than European collectors, though obviously an example as pleasing as this would be an acceptable addition to any collection.

£100 – £125

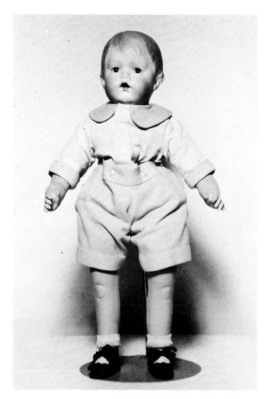

German Bisque
Marked 'J.L. Kallus:Copr. Germany 1394/30' on head. c.1925.
Height 51cm:20in.

An attractive character head with a flange neck and moulded hair. The doll has sleeping eyes and two lower teeth. It was designed in America by Joseph L. Kallus and the bisque versions were made by Kestner for sale in the States. Its name was a combination of 'Bo' for Borgfeldt, the firm that distributed the doll, and 'Kaye' for Kallus, the designer. It is estimated that some 50,000 Baby Bo Kayes were made, a large number with composition heads made by the Cameo Doll Company. This bisque headed example has composition limbs and a cloth body. It is especially desirable as it has all the original clothing. This doll would be of much greater interest to the American than the European market.

£200 – £250

German Bisque
Marked 'Heubach Koppelsdorf 320 7½ Germany'. c.1920.
Height 61cm:24in.

Even the baby type dolls made by Heubach often have the faces of pretty children, as in this doll wearing the original mohair wig and with a reconstructed costume made from old fabrics. It has blue sleeping eyes and the pierced nostrils that are a characteristic of many of this firm's baby dolls, and there is an open mouth with teeth. At present dolls of this type are much more popular in America than in Europe and they provide a promising field for the new collector as they seem very underpriced in comparison with jointed dolls which are often of indifferent quality.

£75

German Bisque
Marked 'Heubach Köppelsdorf'. c.1910. Height 48cm:19in.

A very basic German shoulder headed doll redressed in a printed cotton frock and a velvet bonnet. Eyes are the sleeping type, the mouth is open and the head colouring high. The shoulder plate is cracked down the back and one arm is very badly damaged. The body is of the jointed American cloth type.

£30

German Bisque
Marked '1900-8/0' and a horseshoe. c.1905. Height 35cm:14in.

Made by the firm of Ernst Heubach, a bisque shoulder headed doll wearing the original blue frock, lace bonnet and wig. The body is of the jointed leather type with fabric lower legs and bisque arms. The decoration of the head is not very good as the lashes are poorly painted and the teeth set crookedly.

£65 – £75

German Bisque
Marked 'Heubach Koppelsdorf 399-3'. c.1920. Height 43cm:17in.

A well modelled negro character baby in fine original condition with a brown painted composition body. The brown glass eyes sleep by means of a lead weight. The head is coloured by the painting on of colour rather than the fired on finish that collectors prefer. The quality of the painted finish on this example is, however, extremely good.

£100 – £120

Courtesy Antiques of Childhood, Camden Passage

German Bisque
Marked 'Heubach Koppelsdorf Germany'. c.1908. Height 76cm: 30in.

Some of the heads by Ernst Heubach of Koppelsdorf are modelled with very strong features, as in this example, which give some added attraction to models that are usually of the most basic type. This company was recorded as working in Thuringia from 1887 but few adventurous dolls were made, as the firm relied on the representation of rather sweet faced children. This example has a hair wig and brown sleeping eyes. The open mouth has four teeth and the colour of the bisque is pale. It wears an old peach coloured dress with a white broderie anglaise apron and collar. The body is double jointed. Larger examples of basic dolls have become more popular during the last two years, possibly because new collectors can no longer afford to buy as many items for their collections.

£100 – £110

German Bisque
Marked 'Mignon'. 1918-1920. Height 56cm:22in.

The Mignon trademark was used by the maker Felix Arena and registered in 1918 and 1920. The doll is in completely original condition with a fair wig, blue sleeping eyes and the mouth open to show the teeth. The body is in reasonable condition but the paint is a little rubbed. Original blue cotton, lace trimmed dress is worn and when restrung and the costume washed the doll would be an acceptable example of the type.

£120

German Bisque
Marked 'Heubach Kopplesdorf 250-1 Germany'. c.1900.
Height 25.5cm:10in.

A very small jointed doll of the straight limbed type, with fixed brown eyes and an open mouth with teeth. It wears the original pink and white striped dress and straw hat. These small dolls are now popular and fetch a considerable sum for their relatively small size.

£50

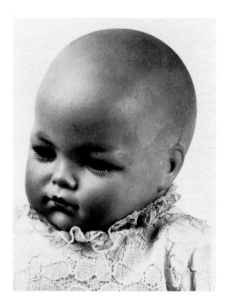

German Bisque
Marked 'SPBH' with a star. c.1920. Height 29cm:11½in.

A bisque flange headed baby doll with an effectively modelled character face made by Schoenau and Hoffmeister. The sleeping eyes are blue, the body is fabric and has composition hands.

£100 – £125

German Bisque
Marked 'S.P.B.H. 4000 5/o'. c.1905. Height 34cm:13½in.

The firm of Schoenau and Hoffmeister worked at Burggrub in Bavaria from 1901, though judging purely by its original costume this doll might be thought earlier than that date. The delicately constructed doll has sleeping blue eyes, an open mouth and wears the original wig. The pin tucked dress is very well made and contributes greatly to the effect and value of the doll.

£80 – £90

German Bisque
Marked 'G 327 B 13M'. c.1920. Height 53cm:21in.

A bent limbed toddler type baby doll probably made for, and distributed by, George Borgfeldt. Many dolls were made to the specifications of this firm by porcelain factories such as Armand Marseille and Simon and Halbig. This example is of a very basic type with brown sleeping eyes.

£75 – £80

Courtesy Christie's South Kensington

German Bisque
Unmarked. c.1880. Height 28cm:11in.

The wearing of Highland dress by the Royal children at Balmoral, and later the popularity of the singer Harry Lauder, made dollmakers continue to costume figures in tartan until the First World War. This example has a bisque shoulder head with a solid crown of the type referred to in the context of French dolls as 'Belton'. The eyes are fixed and the mouth closed. The body is made of kid. Similar dolls were made in Germany by several makers including Kling, and Simon and Halbig. This is a head of very nice quality.

£130 – £145

German Bisque
Unmarked. c.1870. Height 23cm:9in.

Judging purely from the modelling of the face, this doll looks very French, but the type of shoulder head and the fabric body with cheap bisque lower arms and legs makes a German provenance more likely. The costume is original and in good condition and a basket and knitting on needles is carried. The glass eyes are a particularly brilliant blue. While a similar doll in an undressed state would be of only limited interest, this example has considerable appeal because of its untouched state.

£60 – £65

German Bisque
Unmarked. c.1890. Height 14cm:5½in.

A small bisque figure with considerable charm dressed in the effectively made original costume of blue trousers and shirt with a red jerkin. The blue eyes are of the fixed type. Unfortunately one arm is missing.

£20 – £25

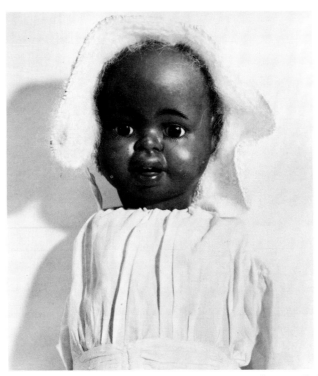

German Bisque
Marked '252 S&Q Germany 46'. c.1924. Height 46cm:18in.

An interesting character baby with sleeping brown eyes and an open mouth, with two upper teeth and a trembling or whistling tongue. Coloured dolls modelled with realistic negro features are only occasionally found and as this doll also has well tinted bisque it is of additional interest. The body is of the typical bent limbed type and the wig is missing. A white baby gown is worn. Dolls marked with the S&Q monogram are known to have been marketed by the Bing Concentra organisation but the author was able to identify the factory with the kind assistance of Francis Bing, who provided a list of the Bing subsidiaries in 1924. This list included Schutzmeister & Quendt of Gotha, thus making attributable dolls to which collectors have previously referred only by initials.

£180 – £200

German Bisque
Marked with Strobel & Wilken trademark. c.1912. Height 18cm:7in.

A bisque headed googlie with well accentuated round eyes of the sleeping type. The stiff limbed composition body is wearing moulded socks and shoes. The doll wears an attractive muslin frock.

£150 – £175

German Bisque
Marked 'R 6 A'. c.1910. Height 34cm:13½in.

A small character baby with a socket head made, it is generally thought, by the Recknagel porcelain factory in Thuringia. The mouth is of the open-closed type but is unusual as it is modelled in a very widely opened position with two white painted teeth. The light brown hair is painted. The blue eyes are also painted. The colour of the bisque is a little high and the quality coarse but the good modelling of the head makes this doll an interesting acquisition for the character doll collector.

£50 – £65

Courtesy Christie's South Kensington

German Bisque
Marked 'CB' on shoulder plate. c.1908. Height 30.5cm:12in.

The mark 'CB' on the shoulder plate indicates that this three faced doll was the work of Carl Bergner. Between 1904 and 1905 he registered several German and British patents for multi-faced dolls. The heads revolve under a carton hood. One of the heads is modelled with moulded tears, another is sleeping and the third smiling. The cloth body contains a voice box. The lower arms and legs are composition. This is an example of very satisfactory quality and the body is also in reasonable condition. A hand embroidered nightgown and a sprigged cotton hooded cape are worn.

£400

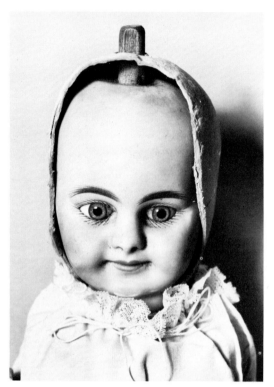

Courtesy Phillips

German Bisque
Unmarked. 1890-1910. Height 41cm:16in.

The smiling face of a two faced bisque headed doll probably of the type manufactured by Carl Bergner of Sonneberg. The other face shows a scowling expression and the head was turned by a knob that emerged at the crown. The blue glass eyes are of good quality and decoration but the doll still retains some dirt as shown in the photograph, which spoils their effect. The cardboard hood, which conceals the unwanted face, would originally have been covered with a frilled or decorated bonnet.

The jointed body is well made but has suffered damage to both the feet and the torso and the complete doll would need restoration before it would be acceptable to a collector. The head fortunately is perfect. All the original costume is missing.

£300

German Bisque
Marked 'G.K' in a sunburst and '44. 15'. c.1900. Height 20cm:8in.

The firm of Gebrüder Krauss is recorded as working from 1863 in Eisfeld and the majority of dolls that can be directly attributed to them are of the jointed and bisque headed type. The decoration of heads from this firm is usually good but this small example shows that standards could vary in the production of a single firm as the decoration and the bisque are of the poorest kind. The body is of the stiff limbed type, whose only movement is at the tops of arms and legs. The shoes are painted.

Although the quality of the basic doll is so poor it does have some attraction because of the good original state of the costume with its lace, braid and chain decoration. The mohair wig is also original.

£40 – £45

German Bisque
Marked '142-2'. c.1912. Height 25cm:10in.

Character babies became popular in the years just before the First World War but they never completely regained this initial popularity afterwards. This baby doll, with painted brown eyes with white highlights, has an almost tearful expression created by the open-closed mouth. The hair is very lightly painted and the brows are also simply but effectively suggested. This doll was made in a wide variety of sizes and was a successor to Kammer and Reinhardt's original character doll 'Baby'. This example is attributed to Kestner because of the number, one of the Kestner series, incised on the head.

£150

German Bisque
Marked 'H 12. Made in Germany. J.D.K 211'. c.1912.
Height 38cm:15in.

A character baby, made by Kestner, with brown sleeping eyes and an open-closed mouth with two lower teeth. The composition body is asymmetrically moulded, with one arm bent to chest level. The original mohair wig is worn and the body, with a voice box, is in good condition. The costume is old and consists of a pink cotton cape and hood with a long white gown and a petticoat. There is a small firing fault to one cheek.

£150 – £200

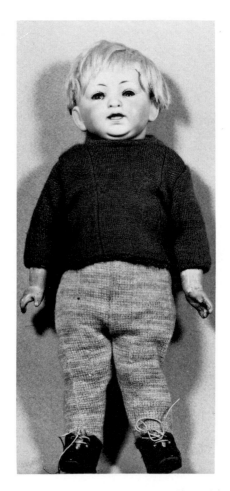

German Bisque
Marked 'B Made in Germany. 162'. c.1920. Height 32cm:12½in.

A bisque headed character boy doll with an open-closed mouth and moulded teeth. The sleeping eyes are pale blue. Kestner character heads are almost invariably of good quality with soft colouring. This head is more usually found on a bent limb baby body.

£350

German Bisque
Marked 'J D K 221 Ges- gesch. F Made in Germany 10'.
Early 20th century. Height 37cm:14½in.

Googlie eyed dolls were popular in the early years of the twentieth century and made in small quantities by several German makers, an S.F.B.J. doll of this type also being reported. This good example made by Kestner has blue eyes and the original wig. The bisque is of the good quality usually associated with Kestner and the colour attractive. The body, of the jointed toddler type with the neater hip articulation, is of the type most liked by collectors. The fine overall condition, combined with the current popularity of all googlie dolls, would make a good price inevitable.

£1,000 – £1,300

German Bisque
Unmarked. c.1890. Height 48cm:19in.

Dolls of German origin with bisque shoulder heads mounted on leather bodies were considerably undervalued for many years, considering the amount of work needed to make the leather bodies compared with the relatively simple structure of a jointed doll. The balance is now becoming somewhat redressed, as the German and Dutch buyers in particular seem to have more appreciation of the work that went into these dolls. This doll, with sleeping brown eyes, is in exquisite original costume and retains the original wig. The lower arms are made of composition. Dolls with heads modelled as in this example are usually described by doll dealers as Kestners, though they are normally unmarked except for a number. The heads are almost invariably of fine quality bisque and the brows are fairly well defined.

The good costume obviously helps set the price here.

£160 – £175

Courtesy Christie's South Kensington

German Bisque
Marked '321 Ges. gesh'. c.1914. Height 40.5cm:16in.

The current popularity of googlie eyed dolls, especially in America, is reflected by the fact that even this very heavily damaged example fetched a good price whereas not so long before many salerooms would have been reluctant to catalogue such a broken piece. In original condition this doll has some amusing appeal with its huge blue eyes, water melon mouth, and sharply slanting eyebrows. Dolls in this very damaged state are rarely purchased by collectors but usually by dealers for restoration.

£250

German Bisque
Marked '151 5'. c.1910-1925. Height 37cm:14½in.

Changing fashions in collecting have recently meant that the character baby dolls which were very popular four or five years ago are now commanding considerably less in real terms than they were then, though they have remained more popular in the States. Dolls with heads marked with this number sequence were made by the firm of Kestner and they were produced in a very large variety of sizes. The open-closed mouth with the tongue slightly protruding and the two moulded front teeth are characteristics of this particular mould. This example wears a white baby gown.

£150 – £175

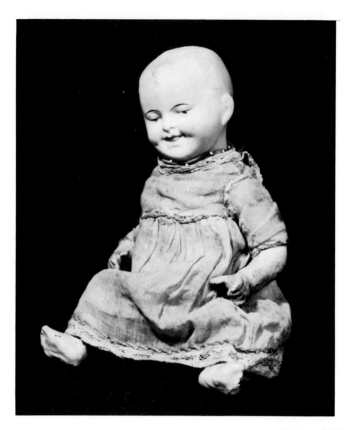

German Bisque
Impressed 'Germany 162-0'. c.1912. Height 25cm:10in.

A character baby mounted on a realistically modelled bent limb body. The head, made of bisque of indifferent quality, has dimpled cheeks and painted brown eyes. The hair is lightly painted in brown. The fact that it is not possible to attribute this doll to any particular maker depresses its value though it does have some appeal. The number 162 was used by Kestner on pretty girl type dolls and indicates how dangerous is the practice of attributing dolls by number, as this doll is completely different and made of a bisque far below the quality used by Kestner.

£100

Courtesy Christie's South Kensington

German Bisque
Marked 'Melitta Germany 14'. c.1924. Height 61cm:24in.

A large bent limb baby doll with sleeping blue eyes and a composition baby body. Most Melitta dolls are of reasonable quality but are usually of the most basic types of modelling. All the examples the author has handled have been of the baby type.

£60 – £70

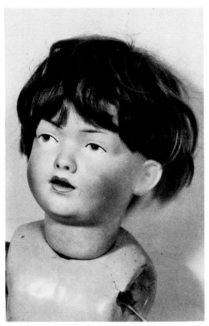

Courtesy Christie's South Kensington

German Bisque
Marked '536 6'. c.1912. Height 36cm:14in.

An unusually attractive bisque socket headed character doll mounted on a bent limb baby body. The face is modelled with great skill and the expression is most appealing. It has an open-closed mouth and the blue painted eyes, with glazed pupils, have a heavily painted line at the lid giving a heavy eyed effect. This doll cannot be positively attributed to any particular maker by the mark and it would therefore be expected to fetch less at auction than its pure quality might suggest. It does have some similarity both of modelling and mark sequence with the character heads made by Bruno Schmidt, a firm that worked in Walterhausen and usually marked its dolls B.S.W.

£240 – £250

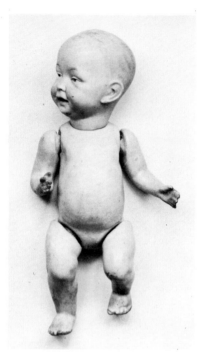

Courtesy Christie's South Kensington

German Bisque
Marked '159'. c.1912. Height 25cm:10in.

A German-made bent limb character baby with the composition arms in slightly different positions. The eyes are painted and the head is modelled with realism. The hair is lightly painted. The number '159' would suggest that the doll was made by Kley and Hahn of Thuringia, who made several character heads in this series of numbers. Their dolls are usually of acceptable quality.

£85 – £90

Courtesy Christie's South Kensington

German Bisque
Marked '830 P. 5/0 M'. Early 20th century. Height 23cm:9in.

The marks on this bisque character head suggest that it was made by Otto Reinecke, whose Bavarian factory used these initials for Porzellanfabrik Moschendorf. The head is modelled with an open-closed mouth, two teeth, blue painted eyes and short hair. The original printed frock and bib cover the carton cone-shaped skirt that contains the clockwork mechanism, which is worked by a key protruding at the hem. Two wheels in the base revolve and small wheels at either side balance the doll as it moves along. Bodies of this construction are particularly associated with figures with Heubach heads.

£150 – £160

German Bisque
Marked 'Germany 6'. c.1910. Height 60cm:23½in.

An unattributable German bisque made unattractive by the replacement mohair wig but showing some potential. The eyes are of the sleeping type and are brown, the open mouth has four teeth, but some of the value is immediately lost by a chip to the eye. The costume is not aided by modern lampshade fringe and furnishing braid, but does serve to indicate how a doll is spoiled by poor presentation. The body is of the jointed type.

£80

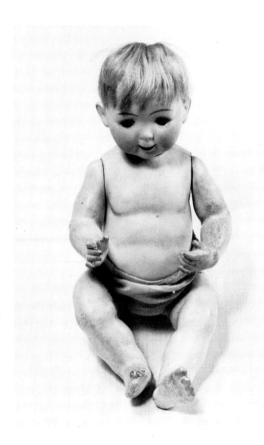

Courtesy Christie's South Kensington

German Bisque
Marked '165-2'. Early 20th century. Height 30.5cm:12in.

An amusing character baby with its original fair wig. The face is modelled with rather rounded eyes and a smiling open-closed mouth that has some resemblance to the so called 'water melon' type lips so liked by American collectors in particular. The price that very unusual character dolls can be expected to fetch at auction in Britain varies considerably, but examples of this type are very highly valued in America and this obviously affects the price an English dealer might pay, though the potential market in Europe is nothing like as wide.

£500 – £600

German Bisque
Marked 'F.S &Co. 1272-32Z'. c.1912. Height 30.5cm:12in.

A small character doll with sleeping blue eyes, an open mouth and moulded teeth, and effectively painted hair. The body is particularly nice as it is of the plump jointed toddler type that is only occasionally found on character babies, but it is completely authentic. It was made by Franz Schmidt, a firm that manufactured dolls in Georgenthal in Thuringia from 1890. The trademark 'F.S &Co.' was registered in 1902. The rather lumpy knitted clothes, more suitable for a bent limbed baby, detract considerably from this doll's appearance.

£150

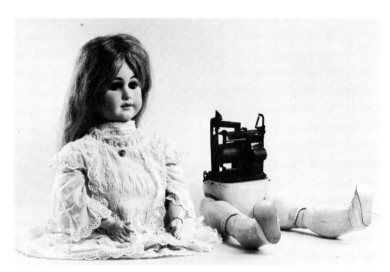

German Bisque
Unmarked head. c.1905. Height 76cm:30in.

The German bisque head of this doll is very attractive and has three rectangular holes pierced at the back. It has sleeping blue eyes, pierced ears and an open mouth with moulded teeth. The composition body has jointed limbs and wears a contemporary child's dress with a straw hat and beaded purse. The phonograph movement is contained in the body and is a reduced version of the Columbia 'Q' or Pathé 'Coq' type, made by various continental firms in the early twentieth century. Small parts of the mechanism are missing, though cylinders could be played. There are no fitting cylinders accompanying this doll. In any examples of a mechanical type the general doll dealer is very cautious of paying a high price for an object that he may not be able to get into complete working order and the lack of cylinders would also tell against the price.

£400

Courtesy Christie's South Kensington

German Bisque
No visible marks. c.1900. Height 27cm:10½in.

Although large numbers of topsy-turvy dolls were made, in particular by the manufacturers of cloth dolls, few were made commercially by the china doll producers. Most examples that are now found tend to have a rather home-made appearance, which detracts from their value. This doll has one bisque head with fixed brown eyes and the other is of composition modelled as a brown boy with blue eyes, red fez and a blue tassel.

£85

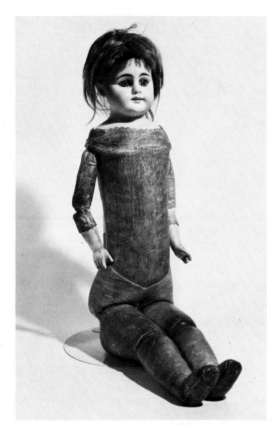

German Bisque
Unmarked. c.1890. Height 53cm:21in.

A bisque shoulder headed doll of German manufacture with the mouth modelled only very slightly open and with good quality moulded teeth. The wig is original and there is a plaster pate. Blue eyes are of the fixed type, the brows are effectively painted and the ears pierced. The lower arms are bisque also. Though the torso is badly shaped, the limbs are gusseted and the legs made of leather, whereas in cheaper dolls the parts of the leg to be covered with socks were often made of fabric for economy. There are no clothes.

£150

German Bisque
Marked 'K & R 117 Simon &Halbig'. c.1912. Height 43cm:17in.

A Kammer and Reinhardt character girl doll with closed mouth and blue sleeping eyes. The jointed body is in good condition and the original cream silk smocked frock and red woollen cape and bonnet are worn. The current popularity of the 117 is reflected in the price.

£750 – £800

Courtesy Phillips

German Bisque
Unmarked. c.1885-90. Height 30.5cm:12in.

A cheap bisque headed child doll with rigid limbs that are only articulated at the tops of the arms and legs. The moulded boots are painted and there is some damage to one foot. The costume, which represents that of a British naval officer, with bicorn hat and sword, is well made and pleasing in effect. It is this costume that the figure will most rely on for its price.

£40 – £45

German Bisque
Marked 'D.I.P.2'. c.1920. Height 28cm:11in.

An attractively costumed character baby doll with an open-closed mouth and sleeping eyes. The body is stamped 'Germany Geshutzt S & Co', Geshutzt meaning protected design. This mark, as yet unidentified, is seen on several character babies.

£170

German Bisque
Marked 'B.P. 585 16'. c.1920. Height 64cm:25in.

A large bent limbed baby marked 'B.P.' in a heart for Bahr & Proschild of Ohrdruf, Germany. The doll has brown sleeping eyes and an open mouth with two teeth. The bisque is an attractive pale colour and the general condition of the doll is good. The original cream woollen pram suit is worn.

£80 – £85

Courtesy Antiques of Childhood, Camden Passage

German Bisque
Marked 'H&B Germany 500/0'. c.1920. Height 30.5cm:12in.

Many dolls are still discovered with the impressed marks of as yet unidentified factories and these have to be judged purely on their quality and interest. This flange necked baby has sleeping blue eyes and an open mouth with a plaster tongue. It was modelled without teeth. The hands are of composition and the stuffed body contains a very effective voice box that creates a howling sound each time the doll is touched. The original socks and muslin napkin are worn. The value of the doll is fractionalised because of the considerable cracking to the side and back of the head.

£12 − £15

German Bisque
Unmarked. c.1900. Height 72cm:28½in.

A large German doll with a smiling expression and heavily dimpled chin. The mouth reveals an unusually large number of teeth which contribute to the amusing expression. The brown eyes are of the sleeping type and the original auburn wig is worn. An effective pale green silk child's coat is slightly large for the doll but could be adapted to advantage. One leg is in a very damaged state, which depresses the price.

£130 – £150

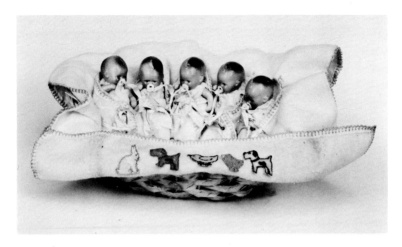

German Bisque
Marked 'Germany'. 1934. Height of each doll approx. 9cm: 3½in.

A group of mass produced painted bisque baby dolls, dressed and assembled probably at home, to commemorate the birth of the Dionne quins in 1934. As the group was assembled from basically poor quality dolls, the group has little interest either as a commemorative piece or as a group of dolls. Had these dolls been direct portraits they would be very desirable. As this is very much an odd novelty item, the price actually obtained at auction is given, though the dolls themselves would be worth only about £25 as a group.

£65

German Bisque
Unmarked. c.1920. Height 22cm:8½in.

A small bisque headed doll with googlie eyes that are not very well defined. Closed mouths of this type are often described as 'water melon' because of the upward curving shape. The sleeping eyes are blue and glance to the left. The body is of the very cheap type with rigid limbs and the legs are moulded to represent shoes and socks. The doll wears a blue knitted frock. As googlies are at present very fashionable, this example would be expected to fetch a reasonable price, despite its most unexceptional quality.

£200 – £250

German Bisque
Marked '109/15 DEP H 6'. c.1885-1895. Height 75cm:29½in.

A large doll with a well modelled head and the original mohair wig. The sleeping brown eyes are very large and the brows are well defined. The jointed body is in good condition, and the doll wears a long white broderie anglaise gown. DEP heads are quite often found on marked French bodies though the heads appear to be mainly of German origin, but of good quality.

£250 – £275

ALL BISQUES, FROZEN CHARLOTTES, PINCUSHION FIGURES AND BOUDOIR DOLLS

The large number of collectors who live in small houses and flats goes some way to explain the popularity of very small dolls, as does the enthusiasm of those collectors interested in dolls' houses.

The fine quality French all bisques, dressed in exquisitely made costumes, well deserve the good prices they obtain, while German all bisques vary much more in price as their quality is uneven.

Googlies, Kewpies, Flappers and Happyfats all have their own specialist collectors, and it is in this sphere of collecting that there is a much wider range available to the American collector, for the early twentieth century German manufacturers put most of their energy into their American export market. Some of the German all bisques measure up to 11 or 12 inches in height and the popular character babies are sometimes made with bisque rather than composition bodies. These characters, in the larger sizes, would be expected to fetch approximately twice as much as similar examples with composition bodies.

All bisques are very susceptible to damage, which has meant, despite the fact that a particular figure might have been produced by the thousand, few examples have survived. Thus, even in a comparatively short time, such a figure could be classed as rare. The highly glazed Bäderkinder, even if quite genuine, are not at present good sellers, for the market has been flooded with good quality reproductions which have cheapened the genuine objects and made collectors apprehensive about buying. The value of genuine Bäderkinder depends very much on size as the small versions have survived in some number. A good quality large example of, say, 15 inches, would be expected to command a figure of around £120 while a 2 or 3 inch version would fetch £5-£10. (Many collectors refer to these as Frozen Charlottes.) All bisque piano babies are collected both by doll enthusiasts and collectors of Victoriana, those with tar or shoe polish dirtying their faces having been generally popular for some time. Because of this popularity they fetch well above the price of an ordinary bisque figurine of comparable date and quality. The value is further enhanced if the figure is attributable. As some reproduction piano babies are now made, it's advisable to be particularly careful before buying. However they are not yet reproduced in sufficient quantity to lower the price of the genuine article.

Reproduction Kewpies have been made for some time and copies were made in Japan when the figures were first introduced. It is only fully marked Kewpies that fetch really good prices, for buyers are apprehensive about authenticity.

Although American collectors have been interested in pincushion heads for some time, they have only recently gained real ground in England. The Japanese versions are not popular as they are usually of poorer quality. They are often marked 'Foreign' or 'Japan'. Figures carrying objects of some kind, those wearing interesting head-dresses, children and boy dolls all fetch more than small basic heads which sell for around £2. The larger versions, in good quality bisque and with articulated limbs can now fetch as much as £18-£20 from a specialist dealer though the average price of pincushion heads is somewhere between £2.50 and £8. They are usually sold in groups at auction as the unit price is otherwise too low. One of the most avidly searched for is the Chocolate Girl, made, among others, by the Goebel porcelain works, in imitation of the trademark used for Walter Baker Chocolate. Male pincushion heads are very rare and a large example would fetch above the top prices quoted.

Early in the twentieth century it became fashionable for women to carry dolls as fashion accessories or to display them on sofas. The figures made for this adult market were usually cheaply produced, with pressed silk or muslin covered mask faces and very elongated bodies, with plaster lower arms and legs. They are not highly popular with collectors but do have considerable period charm and often attract interior decorators. Those thought to resemble actresses, and wearing the fashionable outfits of the period, are more popular than those costumed retrospectively, but it is rare for an example to exceed £25 at auction and most are considerably below this figure. The telephone cover type figures are even less popular, as they were simply torsos mounted on a cage type skirt. The heads are usually made of plaster dipped in wax and the arms are bisque.

Courtesy Christie's South Kensington

All Bisque
Unmarked. c.1870. Height 10cm:4in.

Small all bisque dolls are not the easiest of figures to costume well, so when a pair as thoroughly equipped as these appear, they arouse considerable interest. The dolls themselves, moulded in a sitting position, are of nice quality and fairly obviously of German origin. The boy has short blond curls and the girl's hair is further decorated with a moulded black band. Both have painted eyes.

The main attraction is the number of beautifully stitched miniature clothes which, despite their size, are sewn as correct garments and pack into the small bandbox. The girl doll is seen wearing an embroidered frock with a red and white cape and bonnet. Both have jointed arms. The collector of all bisque dolls would look far before finding another group as thoroughly equipped as this and the price is correspondingly high.

£300 – £350 the pair

Courtesy Christie's South Kensington

All Bisque
Unmarked. c.1885. Height 16cm:6¼in.

All bisque dolls are rarely marked except with a size or a number and many do not even carry the country of manufacture. They tend to be attributed to a French or German source according to their appearance and the type of costume they wear. This charmingly dressed example, wearing a blue jacket and feathered hat would appear to be French. It has fixed blue glass eyes, a closed mouth and a tightly curled mohair wig. The shoes and socks are painted.

The head in this particular example has a bad firing fault at the side, a detail that might cause a dealer a little difficulty in selling. Despite the fault, the general effect of the doll is charming.

£125

All Bisque
No visible mark. Late 19th century. Height 13cm:5¼in.

The original costumes of this pair of all bisque dolls make them interesting. They are dressed as for a masked ball in cream satin trimmed with lace and gold braid. The doll dressed as a boy carries a mask. Such dolls were originally produced very cheaply and evidence of hurried manufacture can be seen in the badly set fixed eyes that would probably need some attention. Some collectors accept cross eyes as occasionally inevitable in any mass produced item and would not consider moving them, while others may reject such a doll in favour of another for this reason.

£165 – £175 the pair

All Bisque
Marked '886 S&H'. c.1880. Height 21cm:8¼in.

All bisques are only very occasionally marked in sufficient detail to be fully attributable. This example can be seen to be the work of Simon and Halbig and has brown sleeping eyes, a closed mouth and moulded yellow boots. The extremely effective costume of pink satin and lace is original and the fair mohair wig is also contemporary. The general quality of this doll is very fine and could hardly be bettered as an example of the type.

£250

Pincushion figures
Marked with numbers. Early 20th century. Height of lady 13cm:5in.

A group of very good quality pincushion figures which are also known as Half Figures. They were often sold loose for home assembly and the most common are those made in the form of eighteenth century style ladies wearing elaborately modelled powdered hair. These three examples are all of an interesting type and would be desirable to any pincushion figure collectors. The glazed porcelain boy with a Kewpie like quiff and accentuated sideways glancing eyes is particularly nice as it also has the usual Kewpie starfish-like hands. It is marked 'Germany 14781' and stands 6cm:2½in. high.

The well tinted bisque child half doll is marked '51442'. The brown hair is crisply modelled with a hole in the top enabling a piece of ribbon to be threaded through. The eyes are well painted and the arms are jointed at the shoulder. It stands 7cm:2¾in. high.

The lady is perhaps the least unusual: but nevertheless desirable because of its great height, and the fact that the arms are articulated. It is marked on the base '1534' though the original arms are marked '3593'. All are in excellent condition.

Kewpie type £20 – £25
Child £25 – £30
Lady £18 – £20

Courtesy Phillips

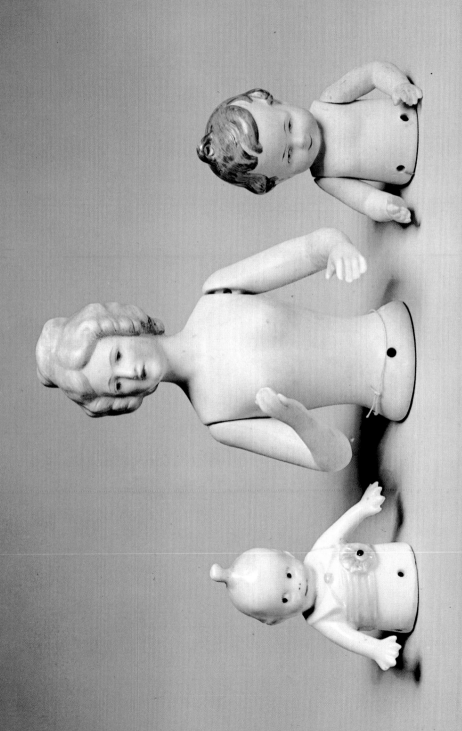

All Bisque
Marked 'Germany 1685'. c.1912. Height 13cm:5in.

The sideways glancing googlie type eyes became popular from around 1908 and many amusing figures such as these were created in particular by Grace Drayton and are seen in rag and composition as well as bisque. It is not known whether she designed this pair, made of a rather coarse bisque and with some of the surface paint rubbed away. They are uncracked and the amusing and very typically early twentieth century appearance more than compensates for the white granular bisque, though in purely financial terms a similar pair in fine tinted bisque would command more than double the suggested price.

£10 – £12

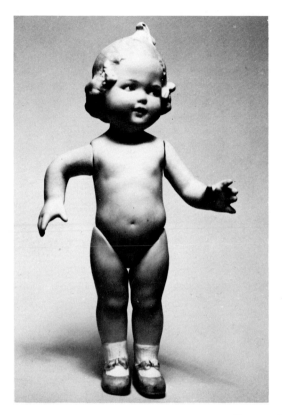

All Bisque
Marked '10490 3' impressed. Stamped in black '23'. 20th century.
Height 15cm:6in.

One of the most collectable all bisque figures in perfect condition and of a medium size. The moulded hair is detailed by brush strokes and the bows are painted blue, the eyes are intaglio and painted brown with highlights. The open-closed mouth shows two upper teeth and one lower tooth. This doll is generally considered to be the work of the Heubach factory, as the face resembles other marked Heubach figures and the number sequence and method of marking is peculiar to that factory.

£125 – £150

Courtesy Phillips

All Bisque
Unmarked. c.1912. Height 15cm:6in.

An appealing all bisque googlie eyed doll wearing a white lace frock and broderie anglaise underwear. The sideways glancing eyes are blue and the head is of the rigid type, modelled as one with the torso. The moulded shoes are painted black and the socks painted blue. One foot is damaged. All bisque googlies are not very common and can be expected to fetch a good price.

£150

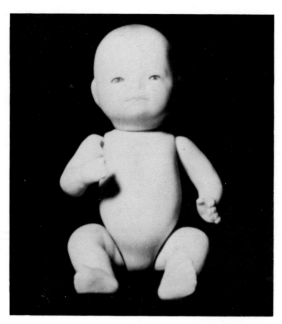

Courtesy Beatrice L. Wright, Phoenixville, Pa.

All Bisque
Incised on back 'Copr. by Grace S. Putnam Germany'. c.1925.
Height 13cm:5in.

The Bye-Lo Baby, one of the most popular of American designed dolls, was created by Grace Storey Putnam in the early 20s. Four copyrights were registered in 1922, two in 1923 and 1925. The artist is reputed to have searched the hospitals in Los Angeles to find a new born child with exactly the right head for modelling. The original model, made in wax, was highly realistic but after it had been modified by the Borgfeldt Company of New York, much of the artistry was eliminated in order to make a more conventional bisque headed doll. Fortunately a degree of characterisation was still maintained and the doll is almost a necessity in any American collection though examples are not frequently encountered in Europe. All bisque Bye-Los were made in several types; some have wigs, others painted eyes, some have fixed heads, others wear ribbon trimmed moulded nappy pants. This example has sleeping glass eyes and a swivel neck and is in perfect condition.

£100 – £125

All Bisque
Unmarked. c.1890. Height 9.5cm:3¾in.

One of the most charming all bisque figures encountered for some time, as both the colouring and the modelling are of a high standard. The head is of the swivel type and moves within a leather washer and the arms are also articulated. The overdress is tinted in a soft blue. The complete figure is in perfect condition.

£100 – £120

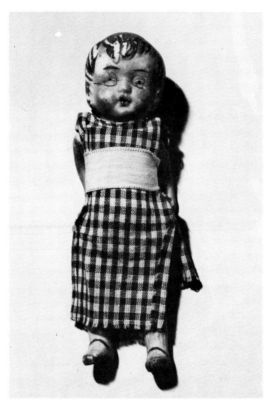

All Bisque
Marked 'Made in Japan'. c.1930. Height 11cm:4½in.

All bisques made in Japan have some interest especially in America but are not much liked in Europe unless of a very unusual type. This example is in a very rubbed condition and has probably lain in the earth for some time. It wears a later check frock and the glasses are painted on the head. This doll was originally a cheap but amusing plaything.

£3 – £4

Courtesy Christie's South Kensington

Frozen Charlotte
Unmarked. Mid-19th century. Height 14cm:5½in.

All china dolls with rigidly modelled bodies are referred to as Frozen Charlottes. The most basic doll of the type is made in a simple two piece mould with the arms to the sides. This doll has well shaped arms with the hands in defined positions. The shaping of the line of the black hair is also more than usually effective. The eyes are painted blue. Very large numbers of these figures were produced in Germany but, since they did not stand securely, they chipped easily. This example is contained in a white German style sleeping bag with green bows.

£30 – £40

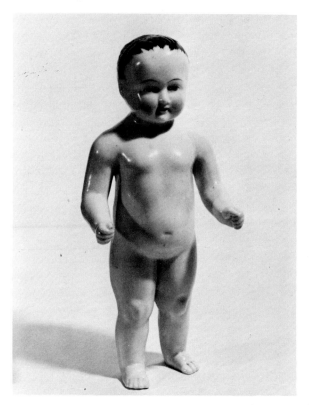

Frozen Charlie
Unmarked. c.1885. Height 38cm:15in.

A well modelled Frozen Charlie of the type made in large numbers in Germany as an ornamental toy and reproduced today. This example has brown eyes and the head some restoration. Dolls of this type are also know as Bäderkinder.

£70

Frozen Charlotte
Unmarked. c.1885. Height 11cm:4½in.

An all bisque Frozen Charlotte with its moulded fair hair held in place by a black band. The socks are edged with green and the boots are gilt. A contemporary lace trimmed outfit is worn.

£30 – £40

All Bisque
Unmarked. c.1920. Height 12cm:4¾in.

An all bisque googlie with black painted shoes. The glass eyes are fixed and the mouth is closed in a tight smile. The bisque is not of very fine quality but the doll has appeal. The original auburn wig and white frock are still worn.

£70 – £75

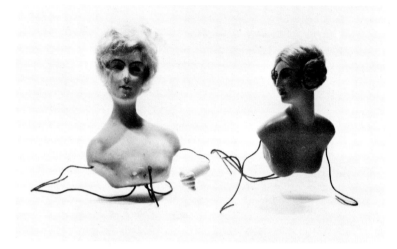

Pincushion Type Figures
Marked. c.1920. Height 13cm:5in.

A pair of figures which were intended to be made up either as telephone covers or even possibly lamp shades. Bisque or composition lower arms were originally wired to the shoulder head. The most elegant head, with the fair hair plaited into earphones, is made of composition and marked 'FEE 9007'. The decoration and modelling of this example is unusually good for the type. The other, of the more usual plaster construction, is marked only with the number '47' and has a chip to the nose.

£10 the pair

Telephone Cover
Unmarked. c.1920. Height 27cm:10½in.

In the days when the telephone was often considered ugly, decorative ladies with long skirts were produced in considerable quantity to hide the offensive device. This example has a composition head with effectively painted sideways glancing eyes and its original wig. The arms, as was usual, are made of bisque. The skirt is wired so it can be placed over either a telephone or a power box on a dressing table. This example is in unusually good condition but since it is in a collecting field which is not yet popular the price is kept very low.

£15

Pincushion Figure
Marked 'Foreign'. c.1920.Height 8cm:3in.

Just after the First World War some German factories marked their products 'foreign' though it was a mark more frequently used by the Japanese. This head, which is in good condition, appears to be of German origin and represents a woman with a yellow ribbon in the hair, wearing a black dress and holding a bunch of brightly painted flowers.

£2.50 – £4.50

Courtesy Phillips

Pincushion Figure
Marked 'Germany 14378'. c.1935. Height 13cm:5in.

A large half figure of glazed porcelain carrying a yellow basket of pink roses. The hair is pale grey with a blue bow and the red dress is edged with gold lustre. Unfortunately the figure is cracked down the back.

£4 – £5

Pincushion figure
Marked 'Made in Japan. Foreign'. c.1930. Height 6cm:2½in.

A pincushion figure made in Japan for the European market. The head is very crudely painted and the decoration of the figure minimal. The hair is orange, the hat mauve.

£2.50

Author

Pincushion Figure
Unmarked. c.1925. Height 32cm:12½in.

The theme of the pierrot was one that obsessed designers in the 1920s and figures of this type decorated a whole variety of items from handbags to fire screens. Pipe cleaners were here used by a commercial manufacturer to create limbs to which pins and safety pins could be attached. The body is sawdust filled and has a round cardboard base; it is covered with dark pink velvet and the limbs in paler colour. The porcelain head is of the flange neck type and has a moulded red comb. The eyes are painted blue. Such figures sat on a lady's dressing table and consequently became dusty and faded, so examples in such pristine condition are nice acquisitions.

£10 – £14

All Bisques and Pincushion Ladies
Unmarked. Early 20th century. Heights 8-13cm:3-5in.

The price of these alluring bisque figures has escalated rapidly during the last four years. They are included not only in general collections of dolls but also in narrowly specialist collections. The more suggestive the pose the higher the price! Some of the figures wear hair wigs and two of this group wear painted stockings. The majority were made in Germany, and belong very much to the era of the glamorous postcards of ladies. The decoration of these figures is usually good, as they were, of course, intended for adults rather than children.

£8 – £25

All Bisques and Pincushion Ladies
Unmarked. Early 20th century. Height 38cm:15in.

A plaster lady's head and shoulders, wax dipped for greater realism. Painted brown eyes are heavily shadowed with purple to create an effective period face which is accentuated by the heavily piled hair. Such heads were often sold loose, together with very elegant bisque arms for home assembly into telephone covers or nightdress cases. They are most frequently found made into telephone covers and given wide frilled skirts. Despite their raddled period charm they are not popular with doll collectors and only command the lowest of prices.

This example was converted into a doll-like figure and home-made legs were added.

£12 – £15

Courtesy Christie's South Kensington

All Bisques and Pincushion Ladies
Unmarked. c.1925. Height 11cm:4½in.

A porcelain pincushion type half figure of a Diaghilev dancer. The stylisation of the figure, with its raised arms, is very effective, and the painted decoration of the costume is evocative of the period.

£25

Boudoir Doll
Unmarked. c.1925. Height 23cm:9in.

Heads of this type were made in the 20s and 30s into a variety of rather useless but decorative items such as this nightdress case. The head, which is of the flocked type, has some damage to the cheek but the long lashes are well set and the turbaned hair style is effective as completely evocative of its period. The hair is black silk. Such items do not exactly fall into the sphere of collectors and consequently fetch only small amounts.

£4 – £5

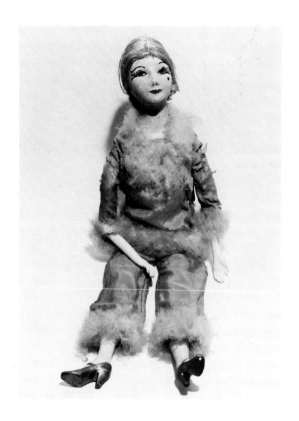

Boudoir Doll
Unmarked. c.1925. Height 74cm:29in.

It was fashionable both in the Edwardian period and in the 1920s for young women to carry mascots or dolls of an adult type when they went to dances or out walking. Since boudoir dolls were novelty items, to be discarded once fashion changed, they were usually constructed very cheaply. The bodies are of cheap muslin or cotton, sometimes stuffed with straw, and the lower parts of limbs, as in this example, often of chalk or composition. This doll has a plaster type face which is basically a mask sewn to the roughly padded head. The shoes are painted gold. The most attractive aspect are the original, though damaged, silk lounging pyjamas trimmed with pink marabou. The eyes are repainted.

£10 – £15

Boudoir Doll
Unmarked. c.1925-1930. Height 44.5cm:17½in.

A boudoir doll with a fabric face over a composition mould and wearing an effective white wig. The eyes are painted with hair lashes set into a slit over the eyes. Lower arms and legs are made of plaster and there is some damage to the top of one leg. The original pink silk overdress and shot green silk skirt are worn and generally the figure is in extremely good condition.

£20

FRENCH BÉBÉ

Somewhere around 1870 it seems to have been decided that children would prefer a doll that itself resembled a child. The French manufacturers were the first to turn from the making of lady dolls to the creation of the heads of very beautiful, idealised children, with large glass eyes of extraordinary luminosity. The type of bodies that had originally been found on lady dolls were at first adapted for the new girl dolls, this development stage being particularly evident in the early dolls made by Bru. The traditional method of wigging a lady doll with sheepskin was maintained, as was the convention of bisque lower arms. Bru even gave their bébés small breasts. As almost every collector wishes to own an example of the work of this firm, prices maintain a very high level, though it should be noted that not every doll marked Bru is very valuable, as some of the later examples are of indifferent quality.

Leather bodies were replaced in the main by ball jointed wood in the 1870s and by an amalgamation of wood and composition that enabled a doll to sit or stand. A number of French firms made dolls of this type, with the simple socket heads, and their work varies greatly in quality. Jumeau, for instance, produced dolls' heads from identical moulds that can range in quality from the exquisite to the frankly coarse. The mere presence of a maker's mark is not therefore a guide to value – so much depends on quality. It is extremely difficult to convey the delicacy of a particular bisque in a photograph, so I have made some indication of the type of bisque in the text. Any damage to the head of this type of doll immediately affects the value, though damage under the hair is sometimes accepted if the doll is particularly fine. Restoration, though helpful, is rarely fully successful, as damage can usually be seen on close examination and the colours used often change after a few years, making further attention necessary.

Late French dolls often have the open mouths with inserted teeth and weighted sleeping eyes usually associated with the German makers. The later types used to be valued very much in line with good German dolls of similar type but recently any of French origin have been fetching a better price, despite sometimes poorer quality. This seems to be because the prices of the older French dolls are so high that the poorer collector is anxious to obtain any examples within his price range.

Some particularly fine character dolls were made in the early twentieth century by S.F.B.J. (Société Française de Fabrication des Bébés et Jouets - the amalgamation of French dollmakers, set up to attempt to compete with the low priced German toys). These character dolls, because of their good quality and comparative rarity, are among the more expensive dolls of the type, the possible exception to this being the S.F.B.J. 236 which seems to have been made in a large number, though even here a particularly fine example can fetch up to £200.

Courtesy Christie's South Kensington

French Bisque
Marked on neck 'Bru Jn 6'. c.1885. Height 47cm:18½in.

Many of the dolls made by Bru are rather highly coloured, but in this example the bisque is tinted delicately. The body is described as wood and composition type with fixed wrists. The head is of the later socket type. The eyes are brown and the doll has pierced ears and is dressed in a red satin frock trimmed with moiré satin ribbon and wears a velvet hat with ostrich plumes. There is a matching ostrich trimmed muff. The shoes are made by Jumeau. It is accompanied by a drop fronted trunk containing an assortment of clothes of the same period but from various makers; the kid boots, for instance, are by le Phenix. Despite the fact that the trousseau was not all created by Bru it does form an interesting period piece, as the equipment was such as a child of the period might have bought for the doll on various shopping expeditions. It would now be very difficult to assemble another such group. The trunk itself was sold by Jouets Simonne on the Rue de Rivoli.

£2,750 – £3,000 (with clothes)

French Bébé
Marked '5' on shoulder. c.1880. Height 43cm:17in.

It is unusual to find dolls of this quality still in their original factory
made costumes. The large brown paperweight eyes enhance the colour
of the bisque which is already delicate for a Bru. The open-closed
mouth is also typical as are the pierced ears and a head that turns
within a bisque shoulder plate. The bisque lower arms have the delicate
modelling of the fingers which is a peculiarity of the firm. The body is
of gusseted kid and all in fine condition. The original costume consists
of a red checked satin frock and a matching plush hat, black stockings,
and buckled shoes marked 'B'. There is also a spare grey frock and a
cape. This classic type doll in mint condition is highly desirable as a
corner stone in a collection of French Bisque dolls.

£2,500 – £2,750

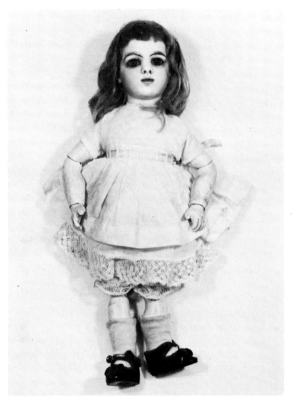

French Bébé
Marked 'Bru Jne 2'. c.1890. Height 25cm:10in.

This is one of the few dolls whose quality looks much better in a photograph than in reality. In comparison with other dolls made by Bru, this is not a particularly exciting example, as the general finish is not as good as buyers would expect from this firm. The painting of the heavy brows is, however, very effective and the modelling of the face remarkably strong, especially when the very small size of the doll is considered. The jointed composition body is of the later type, with separately jointed wrists, a type less liked than those with earlier fixed wrists. Dressed in a more recent white frock, but with the nice addition of the original black shoes also marked with the Bru symbol.

£800 – £900

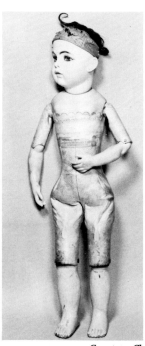

French Bébé
Marked on body and head. c.1885. Height 46cm:18in.

A very fully marked Bru. The head is incised 'BRU.Jne 6' and the shoulder plate '6 BRU.Jne'. The label around the chest reads 'Bébé BRU ... Tout contrefacteur sera saisi poursuivi conformement à la Loi'. The eyes are pale blue and fixed, the ears are pierced and the mouth closed. The brows are heavily painted and the nostrils are defined with paint. The head swivels in a bisque shoulder plate that has moulded adolescent breasts but the nipples are not pink tinted. One eye is badly set, though original, and to restore the doll to its full beauty it would need to be realigned — not a popular task on such an expensive doll. The kid covered body has metal hinged joints at the thighs and the repainted wooden lower legs are hinged at the knee. The upper arms are of kid covered wood and the lower of bisque with ball joints at the elbow. Generally the doll is in good condition and the head and lower arms perfect.

£2,500 – £2,750

Courtesy Christie's South Kensington

French Bébé
Marked with a circle and crescent and '5' on shoulder.
c.1880. Height 41cm:16in.

The firm of Bru worked in Paris and Monteuil-sous-Bois from 1866-99. In the early period various patents were registered for lady type dolls but, like the other French quality producers, the main emphasis after 1875 was upon innovations and improvements in the sphere of bébés. Various materials including gutta percha were used for bodies, and oriental and coloured bisque heads were used to create more adventurous figures. The majority of dolls produced were always of the basic white type so any surviving coloured example is obviously of great interest to collectors. This doll, wearing its original maroon and gold satin frock with a ruched front, plum velvet bandanna, bead necklace and a brass trumpet hanging from a ribbon, is dated by the costume. The quality of the colouring on these fine and expensive dolls is frequently poor in comparison with, for instance, the much cheaper Simon and Halbigs, but in an example such as this, pure quality is less important than rarity. The eyes are extremely bulbous even for this maker and the goitrous neck is also characteristic. The head swivels in a shoulder plate with adolescent breasts. The lower arms are tinted brown. Unfortunately in this example a white leather body was used, which does detract a little from the effect as a brown body would be expected from this manufacturer of very high quality dolls. Nevertheless, the doll is a rare example and would be an acceptable addition to even the finest collection.

£2,250 – £2,500

Courtesy Christie's South Kensington

French Bébé
Unmarked head. c.1880. Height 43cm:17in.

A key wound mechanical Steiner baby. When wound the doll cries
'Mama', turns its head from side to side, moves its arms up and down
and kicks both legs. The mechanism is usually marked rather than the
head. This example has fixed brilliant blue eyes and an open mouth
with two rows of teeth, though one central tooth is missing. The colour
is good and the brows well painted. The original clothes consist of a
baby gown, a carrying cape and a bonnet.

£400

French Bébé
Unmarked. c.1880. Height 44.5cm:17½in.

An attractive Steiner mechanical bébé with fixed blue glass eyes, an open mouth and long fair hair. The limbs are of composition. The mechanism contaned in the torso causes the head, arms and legs to move and a voice box is set in operation which cries alternately 'Mama' three times and 'Papa' three times afterwards. This example has a head of good quality and decoration. A later white cotton dress is worn.

£350 – £400

French Bébé
Unmarked. c.1885. Height 46cm:18in.

A very nice example of a walking and talking Steiner with the usual fixed blue glass eyes, sheepskin wig and open mouth. The limbs are waxed papier mâché and the clockwork mechanism contained in the torso causes the doll to cry 'Mama' and 'Papa' as the head moves from side to side. It wears an original blue cotton dress and a spotted muslin pinafore. The bisque and the colouring are very satisfactory.

£425

Courtesy Christie's South Kensington

French Bébé
Marked 'Steiner Paris FRE.A.15'. c.1890.
Height 56cm:22in.

As the modelling of the heads is so effective, a fully marked Steiner, even if in poor general condition, will always command a good price. This doll is also marked 'Le Petit Parisien Bébé Steiner Medaille d'Or Paris'. It has good quality eyes which are typical of Steiner, a closed mouth and original blonde wig. The body is of the earlier fixed wrist type and is generally in rather poor condition, though capable of restoration. The bisque is of a slightly high colour and the price would obviously be affected by a small chip under one eye. Dolls needing restoration to the head tend to sell at auction to the trade, as the private collector usually finds difficulty in obtaining the services of a good bisque restorer.

£450 – £475

French Bébé
Marked 'R 3 D'. c.1890. Height 63.5cm:25in.

Dolls marked 'R D' are usually attributed to the firm of Rabery & Delphieu, a firm that is recorded as early as 1856 in Paris. The dolls are often characterised, as in this example, by their stocky, rather thick bodies made of a heavy and good quality composition, while the heads are often too highly coloured. This example, however, is attractively pale and has the very dark lowering brows associated with the firm. The mouth is closed, the brown eyes fixed in position and the ears pierced. A replacement French hair wig is worn. Both the body and the head are in good condition.

£750

Author

French Bébé
Marked 'J. Steiner Btd S.G.D.G. Paris FA 7'. 1885. Height 36cm:14in.

Even the shoes on this French doll are original and marked 'Jouets Maison Bail' on the sole. Inside the bonnet is an original price ticket. The lace trimmed frock is also in good condition. The doll has a jointed composition body with fixed wrists and the well made hands are typical of the better dolls made by this firm though the blue eyes are possibly not quite as remarkable as those seen on the very finest of Steiners. The bisque is fine, but the general colour a little high. A desirable doll since it is so complete. This company worked from 1855 in Paris and passed through the hands of several owners who recorded patented improvements.

£575 – £600

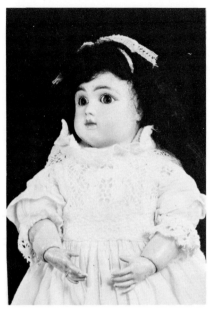

French Bébé
Marked 'Steiner Paris'. c.1890. Height 32cm:12½in.

A bisque headed jointed bébé with a closed mouth and blue sleeping eyes which are worked by a lever situated behind the left ear, an eye mechanism first introduced by the firm in 1880. The head is very fully marked 'Steiner Paris BTE G/SGDG Paris Fre A5', as is the body with the 'girl with a banner' trademark, used after a gold medal was won at the Paris Exposition of 1889, together with the words 'Le Petit Parisien'.

£475 – £500

French Bébé
Marked in red 'Le Parisien'. c.1892. Height 43cm:17in.

This doll is of a much higher quality than might appear from the badly fitting clothes. It is in fact one of the better examples to be included, as the bisque is a smooth quality and a light colour. The brown heavily painted brows are typical of Steiner's work and the original knotted wig is still worn. The ears are pierced and the mouth is closed. This is a blue eyed doll and has a jointed composition and wood body that is marked in purple 'Bébé Le Parisien Medaille d'Or. Paris'. The only piece of the original costume is the corset. The body does not have the purple wash often associated with this maker under the flesh coloured paint. The trademark 'Le Parisien' was registered in 1892.

£550 – £575

French Bébé
Unmarked. c.1875. Height 36cm:14in.

A particularly fine quality bébé with a very pale bisque socket head and
large fixed pale blue eyes with a darker circle around the iris for
accentuation. The original sheepskin wig is worn and the mouth closed.
The body is also of the fine quality earlier type with ball joints at
shoulders, elbows, thighs and knees. The torso has suggested young
breasts and the wrists are fixed. The costume is restorable as the
maroon and blue embroidered coat is very effectively made. The doll is
similar to marked Jumeaus and was probably made by that firm. The
price indicates the much better than average quality.

£750 – £800

Courtesy Christie's South Kensington

French Bébé
Marked '12' on head. 1885. Height 66cm:26in.

The long faced Jumeau is considered among the most beautiful of dolls; in this example the body is marked 'Jumeau Medaille d'Or. Paris'. The bisque of this particular head is of the finest quality and has large fixed paperweight eyes. The ears are separately applied and are pierced. The body is of jointed composition with fixed wrists which could indicate an early doll of the type. The particularly effective head has a fine hairline crack concealed by the wig, so that a reasonable price is still commanded.

£700 – £800

French Bébé
Marked 'L Tête Jumeau 12'. 1880-1890.
Height 71cm:28in.

A typical product of the Jumeau factory, working in Paris and Montreuil-sous-Bois from 1842 until 1899, when the company formed part of the S.F.B.J. syndicate. Dolls marked 'Jumeau' continued in production after the amalgamation but there was a gradual lowering of standard. This example wears its original wig and has the heavily painted brows associated with the Jumeau decorators. The ears are pierced and the mouth is open to reveal the moulded teeth. Although the dress is original it is not very attractive and the underwear is missing. The body, which is of the heavy rather chunky Jumeau type is marked in purple 'Jumeau Medaille d'Or, Paris'.

In this case the photograph somewhat flatters the head as the high colouring, which is unpopular with collectors, cannot be distinguished. The large fixed brown eyes are of the usual good Jumeau quality.

Despite the high colouring and later type of French jointed body any dolls as clearly marked find ready buyers.

£300 – £325

Courtesy Phillips

French Bébé
Marked 'Tête Jumeau 7' in red. c.1885. Height 43cm:17in.

A closed mouth bébé made by the Jumeau factory. The body is in good condition and there are joints at the wrists. The old underwear is still worn, but the dress is recent. The mohair wig is also original and in retrievable condition. The colouring is, unfortunately, very high and the eyes are not of the fine quality associated with this factory. The ears are pierced.

Closed mouth dolls marked Jumeau are constantly popular, though their quality is not really reflected in the prices, which at certain country auctions are sometimes astonishingly high for very medium quality examples.

£325 – £350

Courtesy Christie's South Kensington

French Bébé
Stamped 'Déposé Tête Jumeau Bte S.G.D.G. 3'.
1890. Height 32cm:12½in.

Only occasionally does a very fully marked doll in such effective original costume come on the market. Here a cream ribbed silk dress decorated with gold braid frogging is worn. The original shoes are also marked Jumeau. The head has a closed mouth, fixed blue eyes of good quality and the original blonde wig. The bisque is not very fine and the colouring is high. It can be seen, even from the dolls of this factory included in this guide, that examples of the finest quality are not often found and the colouring is all too often not very pleasing. The body is stamped with the 'Jumeau Medaille d'Or, Paris' mark. The wrists are jointed.

£450

French Bébé
Marked 'Déposé tête Jumeau Bte S.G.D.G. 10'.
1900. Height 56cm:22in.

A closed mouth bisque headed French doll made by Jumeau with pierced ears, fixed brown eyes and original hair wig. The body is of the later jointed type with additional joints at the wrists. The bisque is not particularly fine and the colour rather hectic. The general expression however is pleasing.

The costume consists of a navy woollen sailor suit and leather hat with ribbon bearing the name of H.M.S. Star. Similar suits were popular children's wear in the late nineteenth and early twentieth centuries.

£450

French Bébé
Marked '10'. c.1890. Height 61cm:24in.

An open mouthed Jumeau with fixed pale blue eyes and effectively heavy brows is rather spoiled by the very heavy colouring of the bisque and the fact that the body has been repainted. A later white dress is worn.

£240

French Bébé
Marked '11' Tête Jumeau'. c.1900. Height 66cm:26in.

A Bébé Phonographe with a marked Jumeau head, open mouth, fixed blue eyes and characteristic heavy brows. The body is further marked 'Bébé Jumeau Diplôme d'Honneur S.G.D.G.' The jointed composition body contains a Lioret phonograph movement with a celluloid cylinder playing *Petite Mère Ecoute Ma Chanson*. Lioret phonographs are rare in any form, and this doll would have an appeal both to collectors of phonographs and dolls. The mechanism needed some slight adjustment to put it in working order. If it were not for this fault, the price obtained might be higher. In original box and with instructions.

£900 – £1,200

French Bébé
Marked '1907'. c.1910. Height 74cm:29in.

This is a good original example of a later Jumeau in practically immaculate condition, as it has been stored in its original box with the Maison Jumeau Label inside the lid. The doll's head, in addition to the incised '1907', is marked 'Tête J . . . 14', while the body is also marked with a Bébé Jumeau label. The colouring of the bisque is pleasant and the quality good. The typically heavy Jumeau body is of the better type. A white silk dress is now worn. Though the 1907 is not the most popular of the Jumeau marks, this is one of the best examples of the type that it is possible to find and, in combination with the large size, a good price must be obtained.

£450 – £500

French Bébé
Marked '1907 10'. Early 20th century. Height 56cm:22in.

The eye-catching cape and hat make this doll highly photogenic, but the general effect of the head is not pleasing, as the eyes are very poor quality and the colouring unpleasant. The 1907 dolls are fairly obviously made from the Jumeau moulds and were contained in marked Jumeau boxes, though they are obviously fairly late. This example has a voice box in the torso operated by the walking mechanism of the type used mainly by S.F.B.J., a syndicate that Jumeau became a part of in 1899.

£320.

French Bisque
Marked '1907' impressed and 'Tête Jumeau' stamped in red.
c.1910. Height 53cm:21in.

The '1907' impressed Jumeau head is not usually also stamped with the Jumeau mark as it was one of the later models. This example, of a fairly pale colour, has pierced ears and the open mouth with moulded teeth characteristic of this mould. The brown eyes are of the fixed type and the body of the better French type with fixed wrists. The original Jumeau shoes and socks are still worn. The white lace dress was probably originally worn by another smaller doll. There is a hairline crack to the back of the head. The original mohair wig is worn and the brows are satisfactorily heavy.

£300

French Bébé
Marked 'S.F.B.J 236'. c.1920. Height 51cm:20in.

This is the most commonly found S.F.B.J character doll but with its slightly smiling open-closed mouth with moulded teeth, it remains popular with collectors. Such a head is usually found mounted on a bent limb baby body but this is one of the more unusual in that it has the original jointed toddler type body, which means the doll can be made to stand — a feature in its favour as the doll can be displayed in a smaller space. The body is in good condition and the costume, though probably originally made for a larger doll, could be easily adapted to fit more appropriately, though the old sailor's hat with its 'H.M.S. Thunderer' band is particularly amusing. The head is in good general condition but is somewhat marred by some unpleasant firing faults in the bisque just below the eye which, although not counting as damage, do detract from the appearance.

£175 – £185

Courtesy Phillips

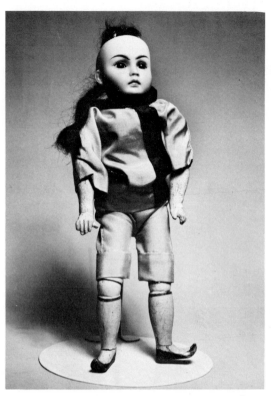

French Bébé
Marked '220 3'. c.1895-1900. Height 27cm:10½in.

An extremely unusual doll modelled as an oriental with pierced ears. The colouring of the head is somewhat heavy, but the general effect is pleasing and the painting of the lips on the closed mouth is particularly good. The brown eyes are of the fixed type and the head is modelled with the full domed crown known to collectors as the 'Belton type'. In this case there are three holes on the crown through one of which the mohair pigtail appears. The body is of the jointed type with wooden limbs and has the very unusual addition of painted Turkish type slippers with upturned toes. The wrists are of the fixed type. Despite its small size, such an unusual doll must be expected to fetch a good price.

£500 – £600

French Bébé
Marked with crossed swords and 'SCH' in shield.
c.1885. Height 41cm:16in.

The mark on the doll's neck refers to its manufacture by Schmitt et Fils, a firm registering doll patents from 1877. Though not as strikingly beautiful to the uninitiated as, say Jumeau, the dolls made by this firm are very much rarer and the prices correspondingly higher. This example is desirable as it is so fully marked, though the head is not very typical of the manufacturer and does not immediately proclaim itself Schmitt in the way collectors like. The body is of jointed composition and the wrists are of the fixed type. The clothes are quite effectively made. The wig is original. The head is of an acceptable colour and the mouth is modelled almost closed with very slightly indicated teeth though there is no entry into the head.

£750

Courtesy Sotheby's

French Bébé
Marked with an impressed 'F.G'. c.1890.
Height 48cm:19in.

Dolls marked 'F.G' are usually attributed to Fernand Gaultier who won a silver medal at the Paris Exposition of 1878. After this time there are other references to silver and bronze medals and in 1889 the firm became Gaultier Frères. A very wide standard of quality is seen in marked examples though the basic modelling is usually satisfactory. The photographed doll has a jointed composition body and wears a very attractive original costume which consists of a purple wool bonnet, dress and coat. The wig is probably a French replacement.

Although this doll looks extremely desirable in a photograph, the appearance is very deceptive, as the head is decorated with an unpleasant heavy pink colouring and the lips are painted in an extremely nasty red that considerably detracts from the value. The painting of the eyes is effective and the brows are quite heavy, a feature of French dolls liked by collectors. The ears are pierced. Sometimes a doll of poor quality in original costume will fetch a surprisingly high price, since a collector or dealer has a spare head of good quality and the same mould that could replace the original and thus create a fine quality example in original clothes.

£300 – £350

French Bébé
Marked 'P.E.D'. 1880-1890. Height 43cm:17in.

Petit et Dumontier of Paris worked from 1878-1890 and it seems that this doll is one of their products. The bisque head with pierced ears is of exceptionally fine quality and has the lustrous paperweight eyes and two tone mouth associated with the best French dolls. The mohair wig is original as is the pink frock and bonnet.

The body is typical of dolls associated with this company, with metal hands jointed to one piece arms. The legs are also of the straight limbed type.

Established collectors would value a doll such as this, of a more unusual French make, very highly, though it would hold less appeal to a beginner who would prefer dolls of a more famous make. The price fetched at auction for such examples is therefore somewhat unpredictable.

£750 – £800

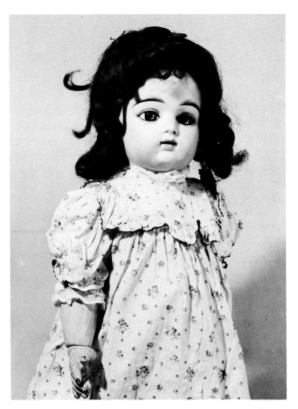

French Bébé
Impressed 'F.G' in cartouche and '6'. c.1880.
Height 50cm:19¾in.

A softly tinted doll with heavily painted brows and large eyes. The lips are softly coloured and the original hair wig is worn. Unfortunately the head is badly cracked. The body is stamped 'Jumeau Medaille d'Or, Paris'. F.G. heads are often found on bodies made by other firms though this is less common on bébés than on the lady type figures.

£100 – £150

French Bébé
Marked with impressed 'R 2/o D'. c.1880.
Height 42cm:16½in.

A closed mouth bébé with a bisque socket head impressed R.D. for Rabery et Delphieu. The heads made by this firm are usually of a heavy type of bisque and the features are also of a very positive type – not necessarily beautiful but interesting since they are so typical of the manufacturer. The ears are pierced and the blue eyes possibly replacements as they are not of the usual high French quality. The body is jointed composition with badly repaired hands. Some damage to hands does not affect price too much but most buyers prefer to acquire the piece in unrestored state. The original white net dress is worn.

£250

French Bisque
Marked with impressed 'Eden Bébé 1'. c.1900
Height 46cm:18in.

The straight limbed body on which this closed mouth doll is mounted immediately reduces its value as it is a simple and economical construction, not particularly admired, though it appears original to the doll as the correctly fitting 'Eden Bébé' shoes are still worn. The blue and white check dress is later. The socket head is made of a rather highly coloured bisque and has pierced ears. The large brown eyes are of the fixed type. A replacement wig is worn. The price of this example indicates clearly that not all French closed mouth dolls can be highly regarded.

£200

Courtesy Sotheby's

French Bébé
Marked with an impressed 'Jullien 12'. c.1900.
Height 84cm:33in.

An unusually large French doll wearing its original costume of a pink sprigged frock and a white sprigged pinafore together with black shoes marked 'J.Jne'. The firm of Jullien is recorded in Paris as early as 1863 but marked examples are invariably of the later jointed type. In 1904 the firm was amalgamated with S.F.B.J.

This doll, wearing its original fair wig, has sleeping brown eyes, an open mouth with six teeth and pierced ears. The body is in good condition and of the heavy 'chunky' type liked by collectors. The colouring of the head is subtle and very acceptable, yet the general effect of the doll is a little disappointing as the appearance does not have that distinctly French effect collectors look for. Julliens do not, however, appear on the market as often as, for instance, Jumeaus and despite the rather Germanic appearance fetch respectable amounts. The doll was contained in the original box.

£300 – £325

French Bébé
Marked with impressed 'Eden Bébé' c.1900. Height 48cm:19in.

This doll is interesting since, as it is in its original condition, it shows quite clearly how shoddily some of the French bébés were originally constructed and costumed. A muslin frock, meagrely trimmed with cheap lace, is worn. Around the hip, is the firm's own ribbon, gold printed with 'Eden Bébé Breveté S.G.D.G.' The body is of the straight limbed type and the doll has fixed brown eyes. The remains of the original wig is worn. The unscrupulous dealer would mount this head on a good jointed body and thus create a much more valuable doll, though its historical interest would then be lost.

£250

French Bébé
Marked 'S.F.B.J. 60 Paris'. c.1910. Height 42cm:16½in.

A very basic S.F.B.J. with the rather unevenly coloured bisque often found on heads made by the amalgamation of firms. The dark brown sleeping eyes were also the type most frequently used and many are found with an imperfection running down the centre of the pupil. This doll has an open mouth with typical French moulded teeth and a jointed composition body. Despite some shortcomings common to most dolls from this mould, the figure is made most appealing by being dressed in a sailor suit and straw boater which will 'sell' the doll.

£125

French Bébé
Marked 'S.F.B.J. 301 13 Paris'. c.1910. Height 76cm:30in.

This is another of the fairly commonly found S.F.B.J. moulds, but this example is made from a good quality bisque and the general effect of the head is pleasing, as the colouring is delicate. The head is of the socket type and has large sleeping brown eyes and an open mouth with moulded teeth. The body is jointed and in good general condition. An auburn replacement wig increases the doll's effectiveness and a white spotted net dress and bonnet with ribbon decoration is worn. This is a good example of this mould and would be found agreeable by the majority of collectors.

£200 – £250

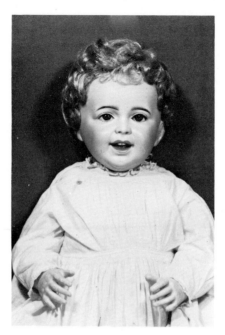

French Character
Marked 'S.F.B.J. 236 Paris 11'. c.1912. Height 58cm:23in.

This is one of the most commonly found character dolls made by
S.F.B.J. The doll has an open-closed mouth revealing two teeth and a
jointed bent limb baby body. The eyes are of the sleeping type, with
effectively painted brows. This is one of the few French dolls whose
price, in relation to the basic jointed bisques, has actually dropped over
the last three years, though this example is good of its type and in fine
general condition.

£225

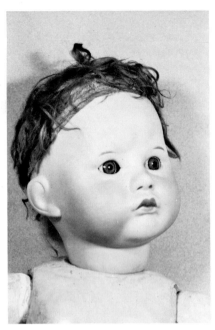

French Bisque
Marked 'S.F.B.J. 252'. c.1914. Height 63.5cm:25in.

A pale and attractive bent limb character baby made by S.F.B.J. with well modelled feet with separated big toes. The head is of the pouting type with a good fold under the sulking lower lip and blue sleeping eyes. What remains of the original fair wig is worn. The rarer characters made by this firm are very heavily collected as the quality of the bisque and the modelling is so effective.

£700 – £750

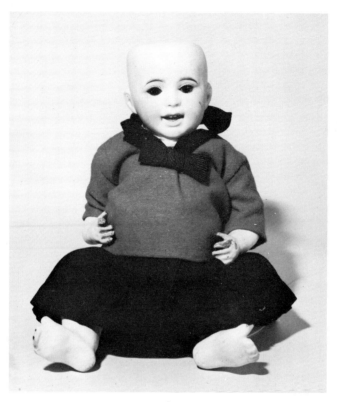

French Bébé
Marked 'S.F.B.J. Paris 236'. c.1920. Height 33cm:13in.

This particular character doll is an example of a type that has actually fallen in price in real terms over the last ten years, though individual dolls of this mould can still fetch high prices if the bisque is particularly fine. This doll, besides being of a small size has the added disadvantage of poor bisque of the rather spotted type so often found on S.F.B.Js. The wig is lost and the mouth is of the open-closed type peculiar to this mould, with modelled teeth. The bent limb body has the original red and black woollen dress.

£180

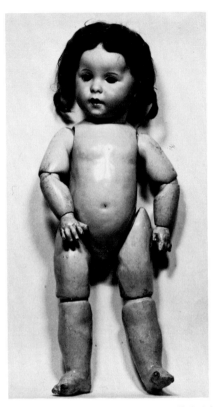

French Bébé
Marked 'S.F.B.J. 247 Paris 8'. c.1920. Height 43cm:17in.

Société Française de Fabrication des Bébés et Jouets was set up in 1899 in an attempt to compete with the lower priced mass produced German dolls. Bru, Jumeau, Rabery & Delphieu and later Danel et Cie were among the members. The quality and collectability of dolls made by this amalgamation vary considerably but among the most desirable are the character dolls, especially those mounted on jointed toddler type bodies. This example has brown sleeping eyes and an open-closed mouth with two teeth. The feet are a little different in that the big toes are upturned.

£350

French Bisque
Marked 'S.F.B.J. 60 Paris'. c.1925. Height 30.5cm:12in.

This particular doll is flattered by the photograph, as the bisque is of poor quality and very heavily coloured. The late French dolls reflect the decline in the industry as standards were continually lowered in an attempt to compete with the effective mass produced German dolls. This S.F.B.J. has the usual dark iris-less eyes associated with this mould, an open mouth with moulded teeth, and the original mohair wig. The jointed body, though of mean construction, is in good condition. A later frock and felt shoes are worn.

£80 – £85

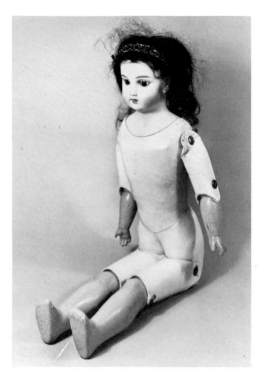

French Bébé
Marked 'A Lanternier Limoges Cherie'. c.1920. Height 57cm:22½in.

The exceptionally poor quality of this head cannot be fully seen in a photograph but it is bad even for a firm which is not generally noted for the good standard of its bisque. An unpleasant purple-brown colouring was often applied, rather in the manner of eyeshadow, around the eyes of some early twentieth century French dolls, which usually considerably detracts from their appearance. The leathercloth body in combination with the brittle type of composition used for the lower parts helps in establishing the date. Brown sleeping eyes, open mouth with moulded teeth, pierced ears and mohair wig.

This type of French doll often obtains almost laughable prices at provincial auctions, as non-specialist dealers often feel that all French dolls are valuable.

£40–£55

French Bébé
Marked 'Cherie 3'. c.1910-20. Height 41cm:16in.

A jointed bisque headed bébé made by Lanternier of Limoges, wearing the original lace trimmed pink cotton dress and blonde mohair wig. The doll has an open mouth and moulded teeth. The emphasised painting of the eyes, giving a somewhat owl-like effect, is a characteristic of this maker and the doll is an acceptable example of a poorer type of bébé.

£90 – £100

French Bébé
Marked 'Dep 10' on head. Early 20th century. Height 58cm:23in.

A bisque headed doll of nice quality bisque with sleeping blue eyes and an open mouth. The original mohair wig is worn but the clothes, with the exception of the drawers, are missing. The shoes are left without soles to allow for the chain drive operated wheels underneath. A voice box is contained in the torso. The head turns and the arms are lifted when the mechanism is key wound. The doll is contained in its original box marked 'Eden Bébé 10 L'Eden Bébé qui marche seul'.

£250 – £300

French Bébé
Marked 'Unis France 301'. c.1924. Height 62cm: 24½in.

Dolls marked 'Unis France' are sometimes found with the S.F.B.J. mark as well, and this was probably a particularly cheap line manufactured by the firm. This example has brown sleeping eyes, but the head is of a very high colour and the bisque also of poor quality, as is so often the case with these particular dolls. The mouth is open and there are four moulded teeth. The lips are very bright red and the costume, though remade, is of suitably old material. Since the basic modelling is not unpleasant this type of doll is always flattered by a photograph.

£85 – £100

INDESTRUCTIBLES

Since china was obviously not an ideal material for dolls' heads, manufacturers searched for another substance with which it could be replaced. Although they succeeded in making heads that were fairly shatter-proof, most were eventual failures as, in time, the surface decoration peeled away or the material became discoloured and even warped or shrivelled. Modern plastics and resins are the most likely substances to stand the test of time and a few collectors are already buying, for instance, the Rosebud dolls of the 1950s as a very long term investment.

Some of the earliest experimental heads were of metal, made either in the form of shoulder heads or later as socket heads. When found in good condition such dolls can be effective, though unfortunately the majority tend to be damaged and they are extremely difficult to restore satisfactorily. Rubber began to be used as a dollmaking material in the middle of the nineteenth century and in America some effective heads were made by, among others, The India Rubber Comb Company. Despite frequent damage, shoulder heads of this early type do maintain some value because of their rarity and because American collectors like to own an example of a type of doll peculiarly associated with their country. Rubber dolls were made later in several countries, but later examples do not command good prices as they are usually too damaged to be collectors' items. Their only value is as curiosity items related to the development of dolls.

Celluloid heads were often used by dolls' hospitals to replace bisque and some very strange marriages are sometimes seen. When it was first used in doll making it was considered a quality material and was used in the making of more expensive dolls. Very nice bodies are often found with rather miserable celluloid heads, the work of Kämmer and Reinhardt being particularly typical in this respect. K & R made some of their effective character heads in celluloid and these, despite their yellowed appearance, are of interest. It is a medium which has only begun to be appreciated recently and prices are still low.

Composition was experimented with seriously during the First World War in America where various combinations of a basic glue and sawdust mixture were used. Horsman had made composition dolls since 1892 when his 'Can't Break Em' doll was patented. Many other firms in Canada, Britain and Germany developed the material, until almost all the dolls made in the late 1930s were of this substance. Most of these dolls now look very ugly and only occasionally does an example occur that is attractive to the collector.

None of the dolls in this section, in spite of illustrating stages in the evolution of the modern doll, would be expected to cost more than a small amount.

Indestructible
Marked with an eagle's head and 'France'. c.1920. Height 25cm:10in.

The mark of an eagle's head was used by the firm of Petitcollin, which specialised in celluloids and had factories in several French towns. This is of the shoulder headed type with a poor quality rag body and painted blue eyes. The colouring is still in unfaded condition which is unusual among dolls of this type. The open-closed mouth has two teeth. The face is pretty and the costume quite attractive, so the figure would be expected to find a buyer with little difficulty.

£12 – £15

Courtesy Antiques of Childhood, Camden Passage

Indestructible
Marked with a trefoil and 'Made in Japan'. 1920. Height 61cm:24in.

Many celluloid dolls have particularly well modelled faces and, created
in bisque, would arouse tremendous enthusiasm among collectors. This
celluloid, with a slightly hurt expression, is among the more successful
Japanese dolls made especially for the European and American market.
The expressive eyes are painted and the body is of the bent limbed
type. As celluloids are so fragile, any large surviving examples of the
bent limbed type are worth acquiring as their potential nursery life was
so short. This boy doll wears an Edwardian embroidered gown.

£12 – £14

Courtesy Phillips

Indestructible

**Marked 'Made in England. Cascelloid. 55 Regd.' c.1930.
Height 58cm:23in.**

Large celluloid baby dolls, despite the manufacturer's intention of making a doll that was more durable than china, have only occasionally survived in acceptable condition. Many celluloids were also destroyed by parents when their potential fire risk was fully realised. They are as yet largely unappreciated by collectors as an inherent fault of the substance was its tendency to change colour – a tendency that Kämmer and Reinhardt for instance were continually attempting to overcome. This doll was made by the Cascelloid Company of London and is therefore a little more interesting as well modelled English dolls are rarely found. The condition of the bent limb body is good but there are several faults to the back of the head and one to the cheek. The head is realistically modelled with a closed mouth and has an attractive expression. It is dressed in the original blue and white knitted sweater and short trousers.

£10 – £15

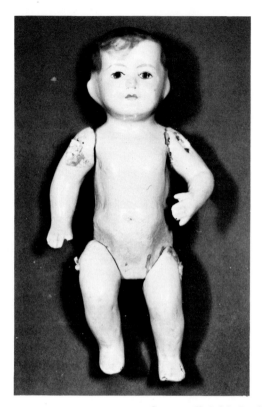

Indestructible
Unmarked. c.1910. Height 24cm:9½in.

This is an interesting example of a doll which, despite its rarity, does not command a high figure. This type of composition is usually found only on dolls of the shoulder headed type and must have been among the earliest of the bent limb type. The head is fixed and the hair is painted in light brown. The eyes are painted as are the brows in a soft yellowish tone.

£18

Courtesy Antiques of Childhood, Camden Passage

Indestructible
Marked 'A.M.Germany 318 /0'. c.1930. Height 38cm:15in.

Composition was used by Armand Marseille very much as a substitute for bisque and little effort was put into the creation of dolls utilising the potential of unbreakable substances. This is a better than average example of this type of doll as the colour lasts much longer in an acceptable condition than similar white dolls. The eyes are brown glass and of the sleeping type and the mouth is open with two teeth. The original white and pink smocked dress is worn.

£25

Indestructible
Marked '201 2½ Germany'. c.1930. Height 38cm:15in.

A composition bent limbed baby doll wearing its original striped pyjama jacket. The moulded hair is painted light brown and the mouth is modelled open with two lower teeth. Though compositions of this vintage sell to some extent in America they still hold little appeal for the European market. At auction such dolls occasionally obtain a respectable price as the bodies are often identical to those found on bisque headed dolls and they are bought to marry with a good head. No doubt in a few years they will begin to command prices more in accord with their often quite skilful modelling but they are as yet largely unappreciated.

£8

Indestructible
Unmarked. c.1935. Height 43cm:17in.

Painted composition dolls are often found to have cracked badly on the surface because the paint and the composition were incompatible. In this toddler type example, obviously dressed by a child owner, the head has remained in an acceptable state though both the arms are flaking badly. The bodies of dolls such as this are not even useful for spare parts so the European value is extremely low.

£4

AREAS OF SPECIALIST INTEREST

There are several groups of dolls which, though they do not arouse much interest among doll collectors in general, maintain healthy prices because they are of particular interest, either in their country of origin or among collectors of very specialised taste. In this context the bisque dolls, made both in England and America during and just after the First War, come to mind, but while some of the American dolls fetch high prices because of their rarity, the British made dolls have remained undervalued in comparison. Neither the English nor the American bisques have much visual appeal so value is based purely, in the case of the American dolls, on rarity. English dolls are usually of a very coarse bisque with rather crudely painted features and their strangely shaped but often original bodies also leave much to be desired. The American dolls have a rather more professional finish.

Japanese dolls made before the nineteenth century are very highly prized in Japan but have only rarely come on the English market where the majority are of nineteenth or early twentieth century origin. Some quite exquisite examples often sell for very small amounts when compared with European made dolls, as their artistry is appreciated by comparatively few collectors. A series of dolls with carved wooden heads was made in the early twentieth century at The Door of Hope Mission in China. These are figures of haunting character and collectors do now seem to be appreciating them. A variety of Chinese dolls, mainly in the form of court ladies and gentlemen, were especially made for export to Europe at the beginning of the twentieth century and this is another example of a type of doll made with great skill which can often be bought at reputable salerooms for well under £20.

Advertising dolls, of composition, printed cotton and paper were produced in large numbers, both here and in the U.S.A. They have a double appeal both to collectors of old advertising material and to doll collectors as, being made of fairly cheap materials, few have survived in comparison with the numbers made.

Paper has been used as a commercial doll making material since the eighteenth century and all types are collected, including those made in the 1940s. Their value depends greatly on condition and those that are uncut or still in their original folders or boxes are most sought after. Besides their costumes, some of these dolls had many accessories, and their value lies in their completeness as well as their condition.

Specialist Interest
Unmarked. Third to second century BC. Height 13cm: 5¼in.

Most serious collectors like to own a few examples of very early dolls, such as this terra cotta figure. There was an established doll making industry in Greece and the dolls, though superficially very similar, have small individual differences. This figure of a lady is very slim and has well shaped small breasts and stomach. The back is similarly well defined. The limbs pivot on string. There is usually some damage, which is acceptable. The face is sensitively shaped and the texture of the hair skilfully rendered.

£100

Specialist Interest
In original box. c.1860. Height 11cm:4½in.

A charming early example of a coloured lithographed doll with four two sided card dresses including a wedding dress and a walking outfit. The original box is still in good display condition which is, in itself, quite unusual, as they are so often battered. The box describes the doll as 'La Petite Élégante'. It was designed by H. Jannin and published by H. Rousseau. Good colourful examples of paper dolls are difficult to find and always fetch good prices at auction.

£130 – £150

Courtesy Sotheby's

Specialist Interest
Unmarked. 1840-1860. Height 16cm:6¼in.

One figure from a pair of mid-nineteenth century moulded sheet wax figures representing a Turk and his wife. They are shown seated cross-legged in contemporary costumes coloured in yellow and green and are protected under glass shades. The man wears a feather trimmed robe and the woman a low cut ball dress. Much of the maker's skill was expended on the complicated clothes and the modelling of the faces was, in comparison, disappointing. Great skill was, however, very obviously needed to create these ornamental pieces and in comparison with this the prices realised are invariably disappointing as such figures do not come directly within any particular collecting field. The skill needed to create a doll is very slight in comparison to that of a wax worker, yet at auction his work can only command about a sixth of that commanded by a mass producer of dolls.

£40 each

Specialist Interest
Marked 'C&H White'. c.1825. Height 27cm:10½in.

Another figure made by C. & H. White, though this time the firm's name is carried on the folio in the doll's hand. The original marbled paper from the base is missing. The figure is of typical construction with woollen hair and beard and a chicken skin face. A blue silk shirt with a cream collar, a black stock and a faded velvet waistcoat are worn. The coat is of very stiff wool with pins at the back to represent buttons while the trousers are of brown velvet. An assortment of wares is carried including beads, braces, cut out leather gloves, boxes of 'Royal Pommade' and 'Pearl Powder' and a music book with the 'Waterloo Dance' on one page.

£180 – £200

Specialist Interest
Marked on base. c.1825-30. Height 25cm:10in.

The wooden base covered with marble paper is marked 'C. & H. White, Milton, Portsmouth', the only known manufacturer of pedlar dolls, though obviously others were commercially assembled. This man has a chicken skin face, common to almost all their dolls, and the hands are made of fine leather. The original costume consists of a red woollen waistcoat, a brown coat and a blue woollen apron. Baskets of brightly coloured flowers are carried. The wig is of orange wool and a printed handkerchief is carried in the pocket. Such dolls are interesting not only to the doll but also to the costume collector, for they exactly illustrate the costumes of tradesmen of the period — costumes that are not often otherwise preserved.

£200

Courtesy Phillips

Specialist Interest
Unmarked. Mid 19th century. Height 28cm:11in.

It seems probable that the head was added to this doll, presumably because the original was damaged. The present head is of the breadcrumb type but is mounted on a well jointed Grödnertal type body which would originally have had either a papier mâché or a wooden head. Sometimes these ugly heads were preferred and one wonders whether perhaps the original lurks beneath! The usual red woollen pedlar cape is worn over a sprigged cotton frock and a white apron. An assortment of old wares is carried in the straw basket including some fans, netted purses and a home written A.B.C. book.

£60 – £70

Specialist Interest
Unmarked. c.1914. Height 43cm:17in.

Bisque headed dolls of this type were made in England by several potteries during and just after the First World War. An American cloth body covers the mark which would be found on the lower edge of the shoulder plate, but there is no doubt the doll is English because of the quality of the decoration, particularly that of the eyes. Both the lower legs and arms are made of bisque and the orginal mohair wig is worn. Many of the German makers had obtained their mohair from Britain so the dollmakers of the war years had no difficulty in supplying the home made product with effective hair. This doll has an open-closed mouth with moulded teeth and the eyes are fixed.

£25

Specialist Interest
Marked on case. 1810. Case 13cm:5¼in.

'The History of Little Fanny Exemplified in a Series of Figures' printed for S. and J. Fuller of London in 1810. This is the fourth edition of a popular paper doll, where the costumed figures were supplied with a single head which slotted in at shoulder level. The costumes here are in nice condition but several of the hats are missing, as is so often the case. The seven outfits are changed as the story unfolds. This example was originally sold by A. Loriot of New Bond Street, London, a shop selling children's toys in the late eighteenth and early nineteenth centuries which was patronised by the royal family — a fact that gives the doll some added interest.

£65 – £75

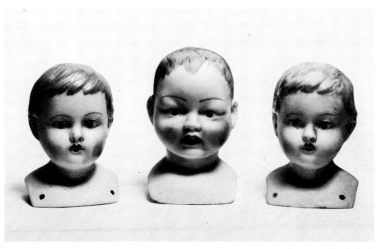

Courtesy Sotheby's

Special Interest
Marked 'Willow'. c.1916-1920. Height 9cm:3½in.

A group of English made shoulder heads of the type produced during and just after the First World War when German imports ceased. The quality of the dolls, with a few rare exceptions, is not good, and they are considered as representative curiosities rather than highly desirable objects. The modelling, as can be seen in the centre head, was often quite effective but the finished dolls were spoiled by poor painting and high colouring.

£30 for three

Specialist Interest
Marked with impressed 'GOSS G 4'. c.1918. Height 38cm:15in.

The British Government felt it would be a bad psychological move for bisque dolls to disappear from the shops during the First World War, as the country's dependence on German imports would have been emphasised. British potteries were consequently encouraged to manufacture dolls' heads and this example dates to this period. The firm of William Henry Goss of the Falcon Pottery, Stoke, had been in operation since 1858 but the manufacture of dolls was only as a result of the war. The modelling of this flange necked head is extremely effective and the artist was obviously attempting to work in the French and German character doll style. The bisque is acceptably coloured and the eyes are painted blue. The hair is lightly moulded and brown tinted. The head is, however, made almost frighteningly unattractive by the heavy red colouring of the open-closed mouth; an example of this type will therefore only be purchased by a very dedicated collector who wants an example for completeness, though it would perhaps be even more desirable to a Goss collector as such heads are extremely rare.

It is doubtful whether the head and body belong together as the hands are fairly obvious replacements and the quality of the bodies used on English bisque dolls was usually very poor.

£200

Specialist Interest
Unmarked. c.1900. Height 29cm:11½in.

Chinese children did not begin to play with dolls until the early twentieth century — doll like figures tended to be ornamental before this. At the end of the nineteenth century figures intended for tourists started to appear, such as this example whose body is built up over a wire armature. The head is made of paper mâché and has painted eyes. Under the wooden base is a label reading 'Made in China. No AJ13.' The rich blue costume is effectively embroidered.

£8

Specialist Interest
Unmarked. 19th century. Height 40cm:15¾in.

A pair of nineteenth century Chinese figures, possibly marionettes, with gofum covered heads and with bodies made of jointed wood and metal. The costumes are heavily embroidered and of obvious importance. The hands are not provided with arms and are simply fixed to the ends of the sleeves.

£20 – £30

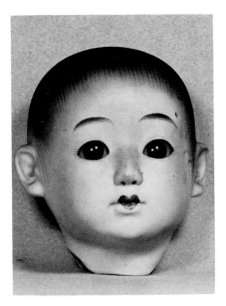

Specialist Interest
Marked with a Japanese symbol 9/3/0. 20th century. Height 10cm:4in.

A particularly well modelled Japanese boy with well shaped ears and cleverly stylised painting of the hair. The sleeping eyes are glass. When mounted on a bent limb baby body this would create a very appealing doll. Despite their obvious quality, Japanese made bisque dolls are not popular with European collectors, so a head such as this would not be expected to fetch a high sum even though it is well-made.

£60

Specialist Interest
Unmarked. c.1900. Height 16cm:6¼in.

A few representative figures from a large group illustrating various characters from Indian society and well costumed in skilfully arranged printed and embroidered cotton fabrics. The bodies are made of a composition substance and modelled in set positions. All are in good condition and are created with considerable assurance yet can only be expected to fetch a very low price at auction as they are as yet unregarded by toy collectors.

£40 the group

Specialist Interest
Unmarked. c.1900. Height 61cm:24in.

An amusing composition headed Japanese doll with inset glass eyes and an open-closed smiling mouth. The ears are very well modelled and the cheeks dimpled. The composition upper body section has painted nipples. The cloth part of the torso contains a squeaker and the grooves holding the doll in an upright position. The lower body and arms are of composition but the lower legs, rather strangely, are wax. The original padded Chinese jacket is worn together with the original hat with kingfisher feather and metal decorations.

£80 – £100

Courtesy Antiques of Childhood, Camden Passage

Specialist Interest
Unmarked. Modern. Height 25cm:10in.

A well made modern Japanese doll with a silk covered face and very cleverly stylised figure dressed in crêpe silk and holding a warrior's helmet. Such dolls fetch very disappointing prices when resold in Europe, though new they are not cheap. The majority of collectors of tourist type costume dolls prefer to buy additions to their collections brand new, so the second-hand price bears little relationship to the actual value.

£3.50

Courtesy Sotheby's

Specialist Interest
Unmarked. 20th century. Height 34cm:13½in.

Despite the obvious skill needed for the manufacture of such figures
they are not at all popular with European doll collectors and are
therefore extremely difficult for a dealer to place. This example, still in
its original box, was in excellent condition though it could be expected
to arouse little interest in Britain. In modern Japan such dolls are
bought as extravagant house decorations and sell for considerably
higher figures than those obtained in the European auction rooms.

£10 – £20

Courtesy Phillips

Specialist Interest
Unmarked. Modern. Height 32cm:12½in.

An amusingly modelled three faced doll made of pale bisque but with very typical contemporary modelling of the features. The bisque is of a rather harsh quality but the general finish is good for a modern doll. The eyes are painted blue. The body is made of fabric and the rather strangely out of scale but original limbs are made of bisque. This doll is sold new in the dress that is worn, but in this case it has been dyed brown.

£7 new

Courtesy Christie's South Kensington

Specialist Interest
Unmarked. c.1925. Height 49.5cm:19½in. and 53cm:21in.

Two puppets with carved and painted heads of some artistry. The man, with dark glass eyes, articulated wood jaw and dressed in harlequin's costume, is an engaging decorative object. The girl, with a head which appears to be of Bavarian origin, is also quite effective though spoiled to some extent by the wooden jointed body which is not very beautifully made. Figures of this type, despite the care that was lavished on their manufacture, often by the puppeteer himself, fetch disappointing prices when included in doll and toy auctions.

£25 – £45 each

Courtesy Christie's South Kensington

Specialist Interest
Unmarked. c.1953. Height 42cm:16½in.

Large numbers of good quality portrait dolls were not made at the time of the Queen's coronation since it was still a period of some austerity, so that a figure as effective as this has some interest. The head and limbs are made of a composition substance and there is damage to one arm. The features are painted and a wig is worn. The clothes are particularly effective and well made. In a photograph the doll appears more attractive than it is, as the rather granular effect of the composition head cannot be seen.

£35 – £40

Specialist Interest
Inscribed on bases. 1896. Height 22cm:8½in.

A pair of realistically modelled wax figures of peasants in completely original state and mounted on stands. A whole range of peasants both seated and standing were made in Central America, where the skill in wax modelling is believed to have derived from Italian presepio artists. Despite the tremendous characterisation of the faces these figures, like those of church origin, fetch comparatively little at auction. In this example the man has some damage. The underside of the stands are marked 'To 'Daisy' Eleanor Margaret with her father's love Xmas 1896' and the other 'To Allan from Columbia Xmas 1896'.

£35 – £40

Courtesy Sandy Morris, Phoenixville, Pa.

Specialist Interest
Unmarked. 20th century. Height 38cm:15in.

The value of folk type dolls varies considerably, depending on the locality of the subject. Those made by the American Indians, such as this example, are obviously of more interest in the States. This doll, with a fabric body and head, was made in the 1940s by the Hopi tribe in the South Western United States. The features and the detail of the costume are created by small beads. The hair is made of wool.

£4 – £6

Specialist Interest
Unmarked. 20th century. Height 38cm:15in.

A striking Japanese figure of a warrior in full armour seated on a prancing white charger and still in its glazed case and protecting wooden box. It was possibly made as a figure for the Boys' Festival, now known in Japan as Children's Day. The modelling of the horse is extremely effective and the costume, made with painstaking skill and care, is certainly eye catching. Such figures are bought in modern Japan as decorative items but are not popular with European doll collectors and are extremely difficult to sell. This particular example is of the better type and should have some market here as a purely decorative object.

£30 – £50

Courtesy Sotheby's